STRATEGIC FORESIGHT

Anticipating and Shaping Future Trends

CONSULTORIA IA

Copyright © 2024 CONSULTORIA IA

All rights reserved

The characters and events portrayed in this book are fictitious. Any similarity to real persons, living or dead, is coincidental and not intended by the author.

No part of this book may be reproduced, or stored in a retrieval system, or transmitted in any form or by any means, electronic, mechanical, photocopying, recording, or otherwise, without express written permission of the publisher.

Cover design by: Art Painter
Library of Congress Control Number: 2018675309
Printed in the United States of America

TO OUR FAMILY

CONTENTS

Title Page

Copyright

Dedication

Brief Overview

Target Audience

Why Read This Book

Preface

The Power of Foresight: Why Anticipating the Future Matters

Tools and Techniques for Future-Ready Decision Making

Scanning the Horizon: Identifying Trends That Will Shape Tomorrow

How to Spot Weak Signals, Megatrends, and the Drivers of Change that Will Impact Industries an

Future Challenges Questions

Creating a Culture of Future-Thinking: Leadership and Innovation

Appendices

BRIEF OVERVIEW

Strategic Foresight: Anticipating and Shaping Future Trends is an insightful guide for business leaders, entrepreneurs, and decision-makers looking to understand and influence the trajectory of emerging trends. This ebook explores tools and methodologies for strategic foresight, helping readers anticipate potential scenarios, adapt to changes, and seize opportunities in a rapidly evolving global market. By blending practical insights with cutting-edge theories, it empowers readers to stay ahead of disruptions and shape the future of their industries.

TARGET AUDIENCE

The target audience for Strategic Foresight: Anticipating and Shaping Future Trends includes:

1. Business Leaders and Executives: C-suite professionals and decision-makers seeking to future-proof their organizations and lead with a forward-thinking mindset.

2. Entrepreneurs and Innovators: Startups and business owners looking for insights into emerging trends and innovative strategies to stay competitive in dynamic markets.

3. Strategists and Consultants: Professionals in strategic planning, management consulting, or corporate development who need practical tools and methodologies to guide their clients or teams through uncertainty.

4. Policy Makers and Government Officials: Leaders involved in shaping public policy, economic planning, or societal frameworks who require an understanding of future trends to make informed decisions.

5. Educators and Students in Business and Economics: Academics, researchers, and students interested in foresight, innovation, and future studies as key components of business strategy and leadership development.

WHY READ THIS BOOK

In a world of constant change and rapid disruption, businesses and leaders can no longer rely on past successes to navigate the future. *Strategic Foresight: Anticipating and Shaping Future Trends* provides you with the tools to not only predict what's coming but also to shape those trends to your advantage. This book will help you:

- **Stay Ahead of the Curve**: Learn how to anticipate emerging trends and position your organization to thrive in a competitive landscape.

- **Turn Uncertainty into Opportunity**: Discover practical strategies to turn unpredictable challenges into growth opportunities and innovation.

- **Build a Future-Ready Business**: Gain insights into how to integrate foresight into your strategic planning to create a resilient, adaptive organization.

- **Lead with Confidence**: Empower your team and yourself with the knowledge and foresight to make informed, bold decisions that drive success.

- **Unlock Innovation**: Foster a culture of forward-thinking that encourages continuous learning, creativity, and adaptability.

Whether you're leading a business, starting a new venture, or shaping public policy, *Strategic Foresight* equips you with the vision and strategies to succeed in an ever-evolving world.

PREFACE

We live in an era of unprecedented change. Technology evolves at lightning speed, industries are disrupted overnight, and the global marketplace is more interconnected than ever before. In such a fast-paced world, the ability to not only predict but also shape future trends is a powerful advantage for leaders and organizations. This is where strategic foresight comes in.

The idea for this book arose from countless conversations with business leaders, entrepreneurs, and innovators who all asked the same question: "How can we prepare for the future when it's so uncertain?" This question, though daunting, holds the key to thriving in today's complex environment. The truth is that while no one can perfectly predict the future, we can use foresight to identify emerging trends, anticipate potential disruptions, and craft strategies that not only withstand uncertainty but also seize the opportunities it presents.

Strategic Foresight: Anticipating and Shaping Future Trends is designed to be your guide on this journey. Whether you are a business leader looking to future-proof your company, an entrepreneur navigating an unpredictable market, or a policy maker aiming to create lasting impact, this book offers practical tools and insights to help you anticipate what lies ahead and shape the future on your terms.

The chapters that follow will walk you through the essential frameworks and methodologies of strategic foresight, providing real-world examples of how organizations have successfully adapted to change. You will learn how to turn foresight into actionable strategy, and most importantly, how to cultivate a mindset of innovation and resilience.

As you embark on this journey, my hope is that this book empowers you to face the future with confidence, not fear. In today's rapidly changing world, those who anticipate and act on future trends will not just survive—they will thrive.

Welcome to the future. Let's shape it together.

1. THE POWER OF FORESIGHT: WHY ANTICIPATING THE FUTURE MATTERS

In an ever-changing world marked by technological breakthroughs, geopolitical shifts, and environmental challenges, the ability to anticipate the future has never been more crucial. Foresight, the art and science of predicting what's to come, offers individuals, businesses, and governments a vital edge. It empowers decision-makers to prepare for uncertainties, identify emerging opportunities, and craft strategies that are not only reactive but also proactive.

While the future is inherently unpredictable, foresight allows us to reduce the uncertainty that comes with it. The real power of foresight lies in its practical application. It is not about predicting the future with exact precision, but rather about equipping ourselves with the tools to adapt and thrive amidst change. The question is not whether change will occur, but how prepared we are for the inevitable transformation that will shape our world. From technology to economics, from social movements to climate change, foresight serves as a beacon, guiding us through uncharted territory with a sense of purpose, clarity, and optimism.

The Need for Foresight in a Complex World

We live in an age of unprecedented complexity. Rapid advances in artificial intelligence, biotechnology, and quantum computing, combined with global challenges such as climate change and political instability, have made the future more unpredictable than ever before. Traditional models of decision-making, based solely on historical data and trends, are no longer sufficient. Organizations and individuals need to look beyond what is immediately visible and anticipate the changes that are coming.

Foresight involves scanning the horizon for signals of change, understanding how these signals might evolve, and preparing for multiple potential futures. It is a proactive approach that allows us to develop flexible strategies that can be adjusted as new information becomes available. This is especially critical in today's world, where unexpected disruptions, such as the COVID-19 pandemic, have shown us the limitations of reactive decision-making. Those who anticipated change were better equipped to adapt, while others were left scrambling to respond.

One key aspect of foresight is scenario planning. By imagining different versions of the future, we can test our assumptions and explore a range of possibilities. This process enables us to identify risks and opportunities that might not be obvious when focusing solely on the present. For instance, companies that anticipated the rise of digital technolo[gy] and remote work were better prepared for the sudden shift brought about by t[he] pandemic. Similarly, nations that have incorporated climate change scenarios into th[eir] planning are in a stronger position to mitigate its effects.

Foresight and Innovation: Creating the Future We Want

Foresight is not just about avoiding risks; it is also about creating the future we desire. [By] looking ahead, we can identify opportunities for innovation that allow us to shape [the] future in ways that align with our values and aspirations. Foresight-driven innovati[on] involves challenging the status quo, questioning assumptions, and exploring n[ew] possibilities. It requires a mindset that is both visionary and pragmatic—one th[at] recognizes the challenges of the future but is also motivated by the potential to overco[me] them.

For businesses, this means staying ahead of the curve by investing in emergi[ng] technologies, exploring new markets, and anticipating shifts in consumer behavior. In [the] age of digital transformation, companies that fail to innovate risk becoming obsole[te]. Consider the decline of traditional brick-and-mortar retail giants who were slow [to] embrace e-commerce, compared to the meteoric rise of online platforms that saw [the] potential for a digital-first economy. The lesson is clear: those who anticipate future tren[ds] and act accordingly are the ones who will thrive.

Foresight also plays a critical role in shaping public policy. Governments that engage [in] long-term planning are better positioned to address issues such as population grow[th], resource scarcity, and technological disruption. Anticipating future challenges allo[ws] policymakers to design systems that are resilient, sustainable, and equitable. For examp[le], cities that are planning for the impacts of climate change are already implement[ing] infrastructure projects that will protect their populations from rising sea levels a[nd] extreme weather events.

Foresight fosters a culture of innovation at every level of society. Educational institutio[ns], for instance, are beginning to rethink how they prepare students for a world where the j[obs] of today may not exist tomorrow. By anticipating the skills that will be in demand—such [as] critical thinking, adaptability, and digital literacy—educators can better equip the n[ext] generation to succeed in an uncertain future. Similarly, individuals who adopt a foresi[ght] mindset are more likely to invest in continuous learning, stay agile in their careers, a[nd] seize new opportunities as they arise.

Why Foresight is a Strategic Imperative for Businesses

Businesses that embrace foresight are more likely to gain a competitive advantage in [the] marketplace. In a world where the pace of change is accelerating, the ability to anticip[ate] trends and prepare for disruption is a key driver of success. Foresight allows companie[s] identify and capitalize on emerging opportunities while minimizing risks that could threaten their survival.

One of the main benefits of foresight is its ability to enhance strategic decision-making. By incorporating future scenarios into their planning processes, companies can develop more robust strategies that account for a range of possible outcomes. This reduces the likelihood of being blindsided by unexpected events and allows for more informed, forward-thinking decisions. For instance, businesses that recognized the growing importance of sustainability were able to reposition themselves as leaders in the green economy, capitalizing on the increasing demand for eco-friendly products and services.

Additionally, foresight can help businesses build resilience in the face of uncertainty. By anticipating potential disruptions—whether they are technological, environmental, or geopolitical—companies can take proactive steps to mitigate their impact. This might involve diversifying supply chains, investing in new technologies, or adopting more flexible business models. The goal is not to eliminate uncertainty but to be better prepared for it, ensuring that the organization can continue to thrive even in times of turbulence.

Foresight can spark innovation by encouraging businesses to think beyond their current operations and explore new markets, products, or services. This type of forward-thinking mindset is essential in industries where technological advancements or shifting consumer preferences can rapidly alter the competitive landscape. For example, the automotive industry is undergoing a radical transformation, driven by the rise of electric vehicles, autonomous driving technology, and changes in consumer attitudes towards car ownership. Companies that are able to anticipate these trends and invest in the necessary innovations will be well-positioned to lead in the future of mobility.

The Social and Ethical Dimensions of Foresight

Foresight is not just a tool for businesses and governments; it has profound social and ethical implications as well. As we look toward the future, we must ask ourselves what kind of world we want to create. Foresight provides a framework for engaging in these conversations, encouraging us to think about the long-term consequences of our actions and decisions.

In a world grappling with inequality, environmental degradation, and political polarization, foresight can help guide us toward a more sustainable and just future. For instance, by anticipating the impact of automation on employment, we can begin to design policies that ensure a fair transition for workers who may be displaced by technological advancements. Similarly, foresight can help us address the ethical dilemmas posed by emerging technologies such as artificial intelligence and genetic engineering. By considering the potential societal impacts of these innovations, we can establish guidelines that promote responsible development and use.

Foresight can help us create more inclusive futures by amplifying the voices of marginalized communities. Often, those who are most vulnerable to future changes—whether due to poverty, geographic location, or systemic discrimination—are the least involved in decision-making processes. By incorporating diverse perspectives into our foresight efforts, we can ensure that future scenarios reflect the needs and aspirations of all members of society, not just the privileged few.

The Optimistic Outlook: Why Foresight Inspires Hope

At its core, foresight is an inherently optimistic endeavor. It is based on the belief that the future is not predetermined but can be shaped by our actions today. While there are certainly challenges ahead—ranging from climate change to technological disruption—foresight reminds us that we have the power to influence outcomes and create a better world.

By anticipating the future, we can prepare for its uncertainties, seize its opportunities, and avoid its pitfalls. Foresight encourages us to take a proactive approach to change, rather than passively reacting to it. It fosters a mindset of resilience and adaptability, helping us navigate the complexities of the modern world with confidence and purpose.

Foresight empowers us to dream big. It allows us to imagine the possibilities of what could be—whether that's a world powered by renewable energy, a society where everyone has access to quality healthcare and education, or an economy driven by innovation and inclusivity. These visions of the future may seem distant, but foresight gives us the tools to make them a reality.

Foresight is not merely about predicting the future; it is about creating it. By developing foresight mindset, we can better navigate the uncertainties of the present, plan for the challenges of tomorrow, and shape a future that reflects our highest aspirations. Whether at the individual, organizational, or societal level, the power of foresight lies in its ability to inspire hope, drive innovation, and ensure that we are prepared for whatever the future may hold.

Understanding the Importance of Strategic Foresight in Today's Fast-Paced World and How Businesses Can Stay Ahead of Disruption

In today's hyper-connected, fast-paced global economy, the only certainty is uncertainty. The rapid pace of technological advancements, changing consumer behaviors, global economic shifts, environmental crises, and geopolitical instability create an environment where businesses must not only respond to challenges but anticipate them. Strategic foresight is a critical discipline that helps organizations understand potential future scenarios, identify opportunities, and stay resilient in the face of disruption. Unlike traditional planning, which often relies on linear trends and historical data, strategic foresight takes a broader view, considering multiple possible futures to inform decision-making and strategy.

usinesses that embrace strategic foresight are better positioned to navigate the complexities of the modern world, staying ahead of competitors and disruptions alike. By actively engaging with future possibilities rather than passively reacting to changes, companies can innovate more effectively, protect themselves from risks, and seize opportunities that others might overlook. This ability to look beyond the immediate horizon has become not just an advantage but a necessity for organizations that seek to thrive in an increasingly volatile, uncertain, complex, and ambiguous (VUCA) world.

The Nature of Disruption in the 21st Century

Disruption is no longer confined to the occasional breakthrough innovation or market shift. It is a constant, driven by the convergence of technologies like artificial intelligence, blockchain, renewable energy, and biotechnology. Moreover, changes in societal values, regulatory environments, and the global supply chain add to this unpredictability. The rise of platforms like Uber, Airbnb, and Amazon are just a few examples of how industries can be fundamentally altered by a single innovation. These disruptions often happen faster than businesses can adapt using conventional strategies, leading to the decline of once-dominant companies.

Kodak, once a leader in the photography industry, is a textbook example of a company that failed to anticipate disruption. Despite being aware of the shift toward digital photography, Kodak clung too long to its profitable film business. It did not apply strategic foresight to understand the broader impacts digitalization would have on its entire industry, including consumer behavior and the eventual collapse of demand for film. As a result, Kodak lost its market position, whereas companies like Canon and Sony, which embraced digital technology earlier, thrived.

Similarly, the retail industry has undergone massive disruption due to e-commerce, with companies like Toys 'R' Us and Blockbuster unable to foresee how rapidly consumer preferences would shift toward online shopping and streaming services. In contrast, Amazon's mastery of strategic foresight has allowed it to anticipate trends like cloud computing, logistics innovation, and the expansion of digital ecosystems, positioning itself as a dominant force across multiple industries.

The Role of Strategic Foresight in Anticipating and Mitigating Disruption

Strategic foresight enables businesses to explore alternative futures through scenario planning, horizon scanning, and trend analysis. These techniques help companies prepare for a range of possibilities, from the best-case to the worst-case scenarios, allowing them to be agile and responsive regardless of how the future unfolds.

For example, scenario planning is a key tool in strategic foresight that enables businesses to consider various "what-if" situations. Shell Oil has been a pioneer in using scenario planning since the 1970s, which has helped the company navigate global oil price shocks, environmental regulations, and the transition toward renewable energy. Instead of relying solely on predictions, Shell creates multiple plausible futures and plans for them. This approach allowed them to stay resilient during the 1973 oil crisis when most of the industry was caught off guard by the sudden spike in oil prices.

Another example is Tesla, whose success can be attributed to its foresight in the automobile industry. While traditional automakers were focused on incremental improvements in internal combustion engine vehicles, Tesla anticipated the shift toward electric mobility, autonomous driving, and renewable energy integration. Tesla's ability to visualize a future where electric vehicles dominate the market, and its aggressive moves to invest in battery technology and software, positioned it as a leader in the automotive space. By the time competitors began to pivot toward electric vehicles, Tesla had already gained significant head start.

Strategic foresight also involves recognizing weak signals—emerging trends or subtle shifts that indicate larger changes ahead. Businesses that are tuned into these weak signals can pivot quickly. For instance, the growing consumer demand for sustainability and ethically sourced products was once a weak signal. Companies like Unilever were able to detect this trend early and embed sustainability into their core strategy, giving them competitive advantage as consumers increasingly prioritize environmental concerns.

Implementing Strategic Foresight: Key Steps for Businesses

For businesses seeking to develop robust strategic foresight capabilities, it's essential to embed this practice into the organization's culture, decision-making processes, and strategic planning frameworks. Here are several steps companies can take to effectively implement strategic foresight:

1. Build a Diverse Foresight Team: Foresight requires input from a wide range of disciplines, including economists, technologists, sociologists, and environmental experts. diverse team ensures that multiple perspectives are considered when evaluating future scenarios. Companies like Google and IBM have established dedicated teams to explore future technologies and trends, ensuring that their innovations align with long-term strategic goals.

2. Horizon Scanning and Trend Analysis: Businesses need to constantly monitor external signals such as emerging technologies, shifting regulatory landscapes, and societal changes. Tools like PESTLE (Political, Economic, Social, Technological, Legal, and Environmental analysis) can help businesses systematically analyze external forces. Trend reports from think tanks, industry bodies, and innovation consultancies are also valuable resources for horizon scanning. Companies like Intel have institutionalized trend analysis processes ensure they remain at the forefront of innovation in the semiconductor industry.

3. Scenario Planning: Companies should create multiple future scenarios based on different combinations of trends and uncertainties. These scenarios need to be regularly revisited and updated as new information becomes available. Microsoft, for example, uses scenario

inning to explore the impact of future technologies on its core businesses, which has abled it to make strategic investments in cloud computing and artificial intelligence well ead of the competition.

Iterative Strategic Planning: Unlike traditional planning, which tends to be static and ear, strategic foresight encourages iterative and adaptive planning. This means ntinuously updating and adjusting strategies as new information becomes available. azon's culture of "working backwards" is an example of this. The company begins by visioning the ideal customer experience and then works backward to develop the abilities and innovations needed to deliver that experience, updating its strategy along way.

Engage with Stakeholders: Effective foresight involves engaging with a wide range of keholders, from customers to suppliers, regulators, and industry experts. These keholders often provide early insights into potential disruptions. For instance, Airbnb's ccess was built on recognizing an unmet need in the market—customers looking for ordable, local accommodations—by engaging with early adopters and understanding ir preferences. By doing so, they were able to create a platform that fundamentally rupted the traditional hotel industry.

Invest in Innovation and Flexibility: Foresight alone is not enough; companies must be ling to act on their insights and invest in innovation. Businesses that are stuck in rigid uctures or over-reliant on current profit models may struggle to adapt. Netflix is a prime mple of a company that has continually reinvented itself. Starting as a DVD rental vice, Netflix foresaw the rise of streaming and took bold steps to transform its business del, despite the risks involved. Today, it continues to innovate with original content duction and interactive entertainment experiences.

e Strategic Foresight Imperative in a Post-Pandemic World

e COVID-19 pandemic underscored the critical importance of strategic foresight, as sinesses around the world were caught off guard by the rapid onset of global ruptions. The pandemic exposed vulnerabilities in global supply chains, highlighted the ks of over-reliance on specific markets, and accelerated digital transformation trends. npanies that had invested in strategic foresight, such as those with strong e-commerce abilities or flexible supply chains, were better positioned to weather the crisis.

 instance, Zoom's sudden rise to prominence was largely due to its ability to scale idly in response to the surge in demand for video conferencing. However, behind its cess lay years of strategic foresight that had prepared the company to meet future nand by investing in cloud infrastructure and ensuring seamless user experiences. ilarly, grocery retailers like Walmart and Target, which had already invested in online ering and delivery services, were able to adapt quickly to shifting consumer behaviors ing the pandemic.

In the post-pandemic world, the pace of change will only accelerate. Businesses must prepare for a future that includes continued disruptions from climate change, digital transformation, changing consumer values, and global economic realignments. Strategic foresight can help companies not only survive these disruptions but turn them into opportunities for growth.

Future-Proofing Your Business Through Strategic Foresight

Strategic foresight is not just about avoiding threats; it's about thriving in the face of uncertainty. It enables businesses to be proactive rather than reactive, allowing them to capitalize on emerging opportunities before competitors even recognize them. The key to staying ahead of disruption lies in embracing a mindset that is constantly curious about the future, open to change, and willing to experiment.

In practice, this means building an organization that is flexible, innovative, and able to pivot as conditions change. It means investing in technologies that will enable future growth, such as artificial intelligence, blockchain, and renewable energy, and preparing for shifts in consumer behavior, regulatory landscapes, and environmental challenges. Companies that take a long-term, strategic approach to foresight, recognizing the interconnectedness of various trends and disruptions, will be better positioned to lead their industries into the future.

Strategic foresight is an essential capability for businesses that want to stay ahead of disruption. By leveraging foresight tools and techniques, companies can better navigate an uncertain world, anticipate change, and position themselves for long-term success. The businesses that understand and invest in strategic foresight today will be the ones that shape the future, rather than being shaped by it.

Aspect	Key Insights	Examples
Nature of Disruption	- Disruption is constant and driven by technologies (AI, blockchain, renewable energy) and social changes.	- Kodak's failure to adapt to digital photography. - Blockbuster's inability to foresee the rise of streaming services (Netflix).
Importance of Strategic Foresight	- Allows businesses to anticipate multiple futures rather than react. - Protects from risks and capitalizes on opportunities. - Builds resilience in a VUCA world.	- Shell Oil's use of scenario planning to navigate oil crises. - Tesla's foresight into electric vehicles and autonomy.
Key Tools & Techniques	- **Scenario Planning**: Creates multiple plausible futures. - **Horizon Scanning**: Identifies weak signals of future trends. - **Trend Analysis**: Systematically monitors shifts.	- Shell's long-term planning based on future oil market scenarios. - Intel's continuous horizon scanning for semiconductor innovation.
Steps for Implementation	- Build diverse foresight teams. - Conduct horizon scanning and trend analysis. - Create iterative, adaptive strategies. - Engage with stakeholders.	- Google and IBM's specialized foresight teams. - Microsoft's scenario planning to stay ahead in cloud and AI. - Amazon's "working backwards" strategy.

Adaptation to Disruption	- Businesses must be flexible and prepared to act on foresight insights. - Must invest in innovation to remain competitive.	- Netflix's transformation from DVD rental to streaming. - Airbnb's early recognition of customer demand for local affordable stays.
Post-Pandemic Lessons	- COVID-19 highlighted the need for foresight in supply chains, digital readiness, and consumer behavior changes. - Future disruptions (climate change, digitalization) will accelerate.	- Zoom's scaling ability during the pandemic. - Walmart's strong e-commerce infrastructure helped meet changing consumer needs.
Future-Proofing through Foresight	- Strategic foresight helps businesses turn disruption into growth opportunities. - Long-term, strategic approaches are crucial for anticipating interconnected trends.	- Companies investing in AI, blockchain, and renewable energy are preparing for the future (e.g., Tesla, Amazon).

2. TOOLS AND TECHNIQUES FOR FUTURE-READY DECISION MAKING

In an era marked by rapid technological advancements, globalization, and constant change, businesses and leaders face a challenging landscape. Navigating through this complexity requires not only strategic foresight but also the adoption of innovative tools and techniques that equip decision-makers with the insights necessary for future-ready decisions. While traditional decision-making frameworks have their merits, the current environment demands a more dynamic, data-driven, and agile approach to ensure long-term success. This chapter delves into the practical and actionable tools and techniques that are essential for forward-thinking leaders who aim to not just survive but thrive in an uncertain and fast-evolving world.

Embracing Artificial Intelligence and Machine Learning for Decision Support

One of the most groundbreaking shifts in decision-making processes in recent years has been the integration of artificial intelligence (AI) and machine learning (ML). These technologies have transformed how data is analyzed, providing unprecedented depth of insight and predictive capabilities. AI-driven decision support systems allow businesses to process vast amounts of data at lightning speed, identifying patterns, trends, and anomalies that would be impossible for human analysts to detect.

For instance, AI is particularly valuable in industries such as finance, healthcare, and retail. In finance, algorithmic trading platforms leverage machine learning to make real-time decisions based on market conditions, maximizing profits while minimizing risks. In healthcare, AI assists in diagnostic decision-making by analyzing patient data to predict diseases, suggest treatments, and optimize patient outcomes. Retail businesses benefit from AI-driven inventory management systems that predict consumer demand, enabling just-in-time supply chain operations.

Moreover, AI's ability to simulate future scenarios through advanced predictive models is a game-changer for strategic decision-making. Companies can use AI to run multiple simulations based on different variables, helping them to foresee potential outcomes and choose the best course of action. This foresight allows businesses to be proactive rather than reactive, staying ahead of competitors and market shifts.

2. Leveraging Data Analytics for Informed Decisions

The era of big data has empowered organizations with a wealth of information, but data alone is not sufficient. The key lies in how effectively data is analyzed and translated into actionable insights. Data analytics has become an indispensable tool for decision-makers looking to base their strategies on concrete evidence rather than intuition.

Business intelligence (BI) platforms have evolved to become user-friendly, allowing non technical leaders to interact with data in meaningful ways. Tools like Tableau, Power BI and Google Analytics provide visual dashboards that highlight key performance indicators (KPIs) and other critical data points, helping leaders make informed decisions quickly. These platforms are designed to turn raw data into intuitive charts, graphs, and reports making complex data sets accessible to all levels of the organization.

Predictive analytics is another critical aspect of future-ready decision-making. By utilizing statistical algorithms, businesses can forecast trends, customer behaviors, and market changes. For example, Netflix uses predictive analytics to recommend content to its users based on their viewing history, which not only enhances the user experience but also drives customer retention. Similarly, in the retail sector, predictive analytics helps businesses anticipate consumer demand, allowing them to adjust their product offerings, marketing strategies, and supply chains accordingly.

3. Scenario Planning and Stress Testing

Scenario planning is a strategic tool that enables leaders to visualize different future scenarios and prepare for a range of possible outcomes. This technique, widely used by military strategists and business leaders alike, involves identifying critical uncertainties that could impact an organization and developing responses to various potential future states.

For example, oil and gas companies, known for operating in a volatile market, often rely on scenario planning to mitigate risks related to fluctuating oil prices, geopolitical tensions, and regulatory changes. By preparing for different price scenarios—high, medium, and low—companies can plan their capital expenditures, investment strategies, and cost cutting measures accordingly. This preparation enables them to remain resilient even when external conditions are unpredictable.

Stress testing, on the other hand, is used to evaluate how resilient a company or system under extreme conditions. Popularized by the financial sector, stress testing has gained traction in other industries as well. Banks and financial institutions conduct stress tests ensure they can withstand economic downturns or market crashes. These tests simulate adverse conditions—such as a sharp decline in asset prices or a sudden liquidity crisis and assess how the company would respond. The results inform decision-makers of the vulnerabilities, allowing them to implement contingency plans to fortify their resilience.

...th scenario planning and stress testing are forward-thinking techniques that equip organizations with the tools to prepare for uncertainties, ensuring that they can adapt and respond effectively to both opportunities and challenges.

Agile Decision-Making Frameworks

Traditional decision-making models, such as the hierarchical approach, often fail to provide the flexibility needed in today's fast-paced environment. Agile decision-making frameworks, inspired by the Agile methodology in software development, promote a more adaptive and iterative approach. These frameworks emphasize speed, flexibility, and collaboration, enabling organizations to make decisions quickly and pivot as needed.

One of the key aspects of agile decision-making is the "fail fast" mindset. In contrast to traditional models that encourage thorough planning before execution, agile frameworks allow for rapid experimentation, learning from failures, and making adjustments on the go. This is particularly beneficial in industries such as technology, where innovation cycles are short, and customer preferences evolve rapidly. Companies like Spotify and Amazon are known for their agile approach to decision-making, constantly iterating their products and services based on real-time data and feedback.

Agile frameworks also encourage cross-functional collaboration, bringing together teams from different departments to make decisions collectively. This collaborative approach ensures that diverse perspectives are considered, leading to more holistic and well-rounded decisions. It also breaks down silos within organizations, fostering a culture of continuous learning and innovation.

Systems Thinking and Complexity Management

As businesses grow and industries become more interconnected, decision-makers must adopt a systems thinking approach. Systems thinking involves understanding how different parts of a system interact and influence one another, recognizing that decisions made in one area can have ripple effects across the entire organization or ecosystem.

In a complex global economy, where supply chains, markets, and technologies are intertwined, systems thinking is crucial for making informed decisions. For example, a decision to shift manufacturing operations to a different country may have far-reaching implications on logistics, regulatory compliance, employee relations, and customer satisfaction. By considering all aspects of the system, leaders can make decisions that are not only efficient but also sustainable in the long run.

Complexity management, a related concept, involves using tools such as network analysis and system mapping to visualize and manage interdependencies within an organization. These tools help leaders identify bottlenecks, inefficiencies, and potential risks, enabling them to optimize operations and enhance overall performance. Complexity management is especially important in industries such as aerospace, healthcare, and logistics, where intricate systems must operate seamlessly to ensure success.

6. Behavioral Economics and Decision-Making Biases

Understanding the psychological factors that influence decision-making is another important aspect of future-ready leadership. Behavioral economics examines how cognitive biases, emotions, and social factors impact the choices individuals and organizations make.

One common bias is the "status quo bias," where decision-makers are inclined to stick with the current situation rather than exploring alternatives, even if change would be beneficial. Another is the "confirmation bias," where individuals tend to favor information that confirms their preexisting beliefs, ignoring contradictory evidence.

To combat these biases, organizations are increasingly incorporating behavioral insights into their decision-making processes. For instance, some companies implement "choice architecture," which is the design of different ways in which choices can be presented to consumers or employees. By framing decisions in a way that nudges individuals toward the best outcome, businesses can promote better decision-making. This technique has been widely used in areas such as retirement savings plans, where the default option is often to automatic enrollment, leading to higher participation rates.

7. Quantum-Inspired Decision-Making Models

Quantum computing and its principles, such as superposition and entanglement, have inspired a new wave of thinking in decision-making. While quantum computing itself is still in its nascent stages, the ideas behind it offer innovative approaches to tackle complex multi-faceted problems.

Quantum-inspired decision-making models embrace uncertainty and ambiguity, recognizing that decisions often have multiple potential outcomes. Instead of trying to eliminate uncertainty, these models allow decision-makers to consider various possibilities simultaneously, weighing their probabilities and making choices that maximize long-term benefits.

For example, companies dealing with complex supply chains or high-stakes financial investments can apply quantum-inspired techniques to explore a wide range of scenarios and outcomes, making decisions that balance risk and reward effectively. This forward-looking approach aligns with the future-ready mindset, equipping leaders to navigate complexity with greater confidence.

In today's fast-evolving world, decision-making tools and techniques must be as dynamic as the challenges businesses face. The integration of AI, data analytics, agile frameworks, systems thinking, and behavioral insights enables leaders to make more informed, flexible, and resilient decisions. As we look toward the future, quantum-inspired models and other emerging technologies will continue to reshape the decision-making landscape, providing even more innovative ways to navigate uncertainty and complexity. Leaders who embrace these tools will not only future-proof their organizations but also position themselves at the forefront of innovation and growth.

Exploring the Best Practices, Methodologies, and Frameworks to Predict and Prepare for Emerging Trends

In an ever-evolving world, one of the greatest challenges that businesses and organizations face is staying ahead of emerging trends. Trends in technology, economics, consumer behavior, and global geopolitics evolve so quickly that only the most agile and forward-thinking companies can hope to thrive. In this context, having the tools and frameworks to predict emerging trends and prepare for them is not merely an advantage—it is an essential survival skill. The organizations that prosper in such volatile times are those that incorporate best practices, methodologies, and strategic frameworks into their decision-making processes, enabling them to anticipate and respond to change proactively. By blending historical data analysis, predictive modeling, and innovative frameworks, companies can better position themselves for the opportunities and challenges that lie ahead. This chapter delves into the best practices, proven methodologies, and strategic frameworks that allow organizations to detect, predict, and prepare for emerging trends.

The Role of Predictive Analytics in Trend Forecasting

Predictive analytics has emerged as a cornerstone of modern trend forecasting, leveraging historical data to anticipate future outcomes. Companies across industries are utilizing machine learning algorithms and statistical models to extract insights from enormous datasets, enabling them to predict consumer behavior, market fluctuations, and even geopolitical changes. Predictive analytics tools like SAS, IBM's SPSS, and Google Analytics not only help identify patterns but also predict when and how trends will unfold, allowing companies to make informed decisions.

A clear example of this can be seen in the retail industry, where predictive analytics is used extensively to anticipate consumer demand. For instance, major retailers such as Walmart and Amazon use sophisticated algorithms to track purchasing behavior, inventory levels, and market conditions, allowing them to adjust their product offerings in real-time. When a sudden increase in the demand for a particular product is detected, predictive models allow these retailers to react swiftly, restocking shelves, adjusting prices, and launching targeted marketing campaigns. This capability to respond rapidly to emerging consumer preferences not only enhances customer satisfaction but also maximizes sales.

Similarly, in the healthcare sector, predictive analytics has proven invaluable in anticipating disease outbreaks, optimizing resource allocation, and improving patient care. Hospitals and healthcare providers use predictive models to estimate patient admission, ensuring that staffing levels and resource availability align with expected demand. During the COVID-19 pandemic, predictive analytics helped governments and healthcare systems anticipate surges in cases, enabling them to take preemptive measures such as expanding ICU capacity and ramping up vaccine distribution.

2. Scenario Planning: Preparing for Multiple Possible Futures

Scenario planning is another indispensable methodology for predicting and preparing for emerging trends. This technique involves envisioning multiple future scenarios based on varying assumptions about key uncertainties. Instead of focusing on a single forecast, scenario planning encourages organizations to prepare for a range of possible outcomes, allowing them to remain flexible and responsive to whatever the future holds.

One industry that has long relied on scenario planning is the energy sector. Oil companies, for example, use scenario planning to anticipate changes in global oil prices, shifts in regulatory frameworks, and the impact of environmental policies. In the early 2000s, Royal Dutch Shell famously developed a series of scenarios to explore the future of energy markets, considering factors such as geopolitical instability, advances in renewable energy technology, and changing consumer preferences. By preparing for both optimistic and pessimistic scenarios, Shell was able to navigate periods of volatility with greater agility, adjusting its investment strategies and resource allocations to maintain profitability.

Similarly, technology companies have embraced scenario planning to prepare for rapid changes in the digital landscape. Microsoft, for instance, uses this approach to anticipate shifts in consumer behavior, regulatory developments, and technological advancements. By considering a wide range of possibilities—such as the proliferation of 5G, the rise of AI, or the emergence of new cybersecurity threats—Microsoft can develop contingency plans and position itself to capitalize on new opportunities as they arise.

3. Agile Methodology: Adapting to Emerging Trends in Real-Time

Agility has become a buzzword in recent years, but for good reason—agile methodology is one of the most effective ways to stay ahead of emerging trends in a fast-paced environment. Originally developed for software development, agile methodology emphasizes iterative progress, cross-functional collaboration, and the ability to adapt quickly to changing conditions. By applying these principles to trend forecasting and strategic planning, organizations can ensure that they are always ready to pivot in response to new information or shifting market dynamics.

One of the core tenets of agile methodology is the concept of "sprints," which are short, focused periods of work aimed at achieving specific objectives. In the context of trend forecasting, organizations can use sprints to gather data, test hypotheses, and develop strategies in real-time. For example, a company that detects a sudden change in consumer preferences can quickly assemble a cross-functional team to analyze the trend, develop a response strategy, and implement it within a matter of weeks or even days. This ability to move swiftly from analysis to action gives agile organizations a significant advantage over their more rigid, hierarchical competitors.

A prime example of agile methodology in action can be found in the automotive industry, where companies like Tesla have redefined the traditional approach to product development. Rather than adhering to the long product development cycles typical of the industry, Tesla uses agile principles to continuously update its vehicles based on customer feedback and emerging trends in technology. For instance, when Tesla recognized the growing importance of autonomous driving technology, the company quickly integrated AI and machine learning into its vehicles, making continuous improvements through over-the-air software updates. This approach has allowed Tesla to remain at the forefront of innovation, while more traditional automakers have struggled to keep pace.

Design Thinking: Innovating in Response to Emerging Trends

Design thinking is another methodology that is increasingly being used to predict and prepare for emerging trends. This human-centered approach to innovation encourages organizations to understand the needs, behaviors, and preferences of their customers, then design solutions that address those needs. By fostering empathy, experimentation, and collaboration, design thinking helps organizations anticipate and respond to emerging trends in ways that are both creative and customer-centric.

A well-known example of design thinking in action is the development of Airbnb. In its early days, the company faced the challenge of attracting users to its platform. By applying design thinking principles, Airbnb's founders immersed themselves in the experience of their potential users, staying in host homes, and gathering feedback to better understand the pain points and desires of both hosts and guests. This insight led to the creation of features that enhanced the user experience, such as a streamlined booking process and personalized recommendations. As a result, Airbnb was able to tap into the emerging trend of the sharing economy, disrupting the traditional hospitality industry and becoming a global leader in short-term rentals.

In the financial services sector, companies are also using design thinking to respond to emerging trends in fintech and digital banking. For example, Capital One has embraced design thinking to reimagine the customer experience in banking, developing user-friendly mobile apps and digital platforms that cater to the preferences of tech-savvy consumers. By placing the customer at the center of their innovation process, Capital One has been able to anticipate shifts in consumer behavior and stay ahead of the curve in an increasingly competitive market.

5. Environmental Scanning and Trend Analysis

Environmental scanning is a strategic process that involves monitoring external factors—such as economic, social, technological, and political trends—that could impact an organization's operations and long-term goals. By systematically scanning the environment for signs of change, companies can identify emerging trends early on and take proactive measures to address them. This process is often combined with trend analysis, which involves identifying patterns in historical data to predict future developments.

One of the best practices in environmental scanning is the use of PESTLE analysis, which examines the political, economic, social, technological, legal, and environmental factors that could affect an organization. For instance, a company in the automotive industry might use PESTLE analysis to monitor government regulations related to emissions standards, technological advancements in electric vehicles, and shifts in consumer attitudes toward sustainability. By keeping a close eye on these external factors, the company can make informed decisions about where to invest in research and development, how to position its products, and what strategies to adopt in response to changing market conditions.

A prime example of effective environmental scanning can be seen in the global fast-food industry. Companies like McDonald's and Starbucks regularly conduct environmental scans to stay attuned to emerging trends in consumer behavior, such as the growing demand for plant-based food options. By identifying this trend early, McDonald's was able to introduce its McPlant burger, while Starbucks launched a range of dairy-free alternatives and plant-based menu items. These proactive measures allowed both companies to tap into the growing consumer preference for healthier, more sustainable food choices, while competitors who failed to anticipate the trend were left scrambling to catch up.

6. Strategic Foresight and Future Mapping

Strategic foresight is a discipline that involves exploring possible future scenarios and preparing for them in a structured way. This methodology goes beyond traditional forecasting by considering not only what is likely to happen but also what is possible. By using tools such as future mapping, organizations can create visual representations of potential futures, helping them to identify opportunities, challenges, and risks that may lie ahead.

One of the most powerful tools in strategic foresight is the use of "wild cards" or low-probability, high-impact events. These are unpredictable events that could dramatically alter the course of an industry or the global economy. The COVID-19 pandemic is a prime example of a wild card event that took many organizations by surprise. However, those companies that had engaged in strategic foresight and prepared for such eventualities were better equipped to navigate the crisis. For example, companies with robust digital infrastructure and flexible supply chains were able to quickly adapt to remote work and e-commerce, while those that had not anticipated the shift struggled to stay afloat.

notable example of strategic foresight in action can be found in the technology sector, where companies like IBM and Intel use future mapping to anticipate the impact of emerging technologies such as quantum computing and artificial intelligence. By mapping out multiple potential futures, these companies can explore various scenarios, identify the strategic moves needed to stay competitive, and develop contingency plans to address potential risks.

These best practices, methodologies, and frameworks form the bedrock of effective trend forecasting and preparedness strategies. By incorporating predictive analytics, scenario planning, agile methodology, design thinking, environmental scanning, and strategic foresight into their decision-making processes, organizations can stay ahead of emerging trends and position themselves for success in an increasingly complex and unpredictable world.

The following are three main themes in which expectations, based on the practices and methodologies outlined, have yet to be fully realized:

Widespread Adoption of Predictive Analytics for Strategic Decision-Making

While predictive analytics has shown immense potential in various industries, its widespread adoption across sectors remains limited. Many organizations still rely on traditional decision-making processes without fully integrating predictive models that could enhance foresight and agility. Several companies struggle with data quality, insufficient data integration, or a lack of skilled personnel to interpret analytics effectively. Until businesses universally recognize the value of data-driven decision-making and overcome these barriers, the full potential of predictive analytics in trend forecasting will remain underutilized.

Real-Time Adaptation through Agile Methodology

Though agile methodology has proven to be highly effective in software development and tech industries, many organizations, particularly in more traditional sectors, have yet to fully embrace its principles for strategic adaptation. Companies may face internal resistance to change, entrenched in hierarchical structures that limit rapid decision-making and flexibility. Without greater cultural shifts towards cross-functional collaboration and continuous iteration, the real-time adaptability promised by agile methodologies will not reach its full potential across industries.

Effective Scenario Planning for Long-Term, Unpredictable Disruptions

While scenario planning is recognized as a vital tool for preparing for a range of possible futures, many organizations still struggle to adequately prepare for highly unpredictable, disruptive events—like the COVID-19 pandemic or future geopolitical crises. Despite the clear benefits, companies often focus on more likely or immediate scenarios, failing to invest enough in the low-probability, high-impact events that could severely affect their operations. Until organizations integrate comprehensive scenario planning with strong contingency frameworks, they will continue to fall short in fully addressing unpredictable long-term disruptions.

These themes underscore the gap between theoretical best practices and their full practical implementation in predicting and preparing for emerging trends.

3. SCANNING THE HORIZON: IDENTIFYING TRENDS THAT WILL SHAPE TOMORROW

In a world of constant change and accelerating innovation, identifying emerging trends is not just an intellectual exercise; it's a survival strategy. The pace of technological, social, and economic shifts means that the future is not a distant concept but an evolving reality. Leaders, businesses, and individuals must become adept at scanning the horizon to anticipate the developments that will shape tomorrow. By understanding these trends today, we position ourselves to harness new opportunities, mitigate risks, and drive meaningful change. But how do we effectively recognize these trends, and what should we be looking for as we peer into the future?

The Power of Early Trend Identification

The ability to identify trends early offers a competitive advantage, one that can define success or failure. In the business world, companies that have been early adopters of new technologies—think of Apple with the iPhone, Amazon with e-commerce, or Tesla with electric vehicles—have managed to leapfrog competitors and establish themselves as market leaders. This process is not about merely following fads; it requires a nuanced understanding of where the world is headed and acting decisively when the signs are still unclear.

Being able to scan the horizon for emerging trends requires a broad perspective, the willingness to question assumptions, and the capacity to synthesize information from a wide range of sources. It's about recognizing weak signals—those subtle indicators that something significant is about to change—and then connecting the dots between seemingly unrelated developments.

Let's explore some of the most transformative trends on the horizon that are poised to reshape industries, societies, and even our everyday lives in the near future.

The Evolution of Artificial Intelligence (AI)

Artificial Intelligence (AI) is no longer just a tool for automating repetitive tasks or analyzing large data sets; it's evolving into a foundational technology that will redefine how we work, learn, and live. Already, AI is powering advancements in healthcare, finance, and education. We've seen AI algorithms used in diagnosing diseases more accurately than human doctors, and in financial markets, AI is driving high-frequency trading and fraud detection.

The next phase of AI evolution, however, is even more revolutionary. We're on the cusp of developing AI systems capable of understanding and processing human language at near human levels. This is where technologies like natural language processing (NLP) come in, which will allow machines to interact with humans more seamlessly and intelligently. AI will become more integrated into our daily lives, functioning as personal assistants, advisors, and problem-solvers.

Consider the impact on industries like customer service and sales. AI-driven chatbots and virtual agents are already transforming customer interactions, providing round-the-clock support, personalized recommendations, and quick resolutions to queries. The cost savings for businesses are significant, but more importantly, the user experience is set to improve dramatically as AI becomes more adept at mimicking human-like empathy and intuition.

In education, AI will revolutionize how we teach and learn. Adaptive learning platforms that tailor educational content to the needs of each student are just the beginning. Imagine AI systems that act as personalized tutors, capable of monitoring a student's learning progress and adjusting instruction in real time based on their understanding and retention. This could democratize education, making high-quality learning accessible to anyone with an internet connection.

2. The Shift to Remote and Hybrid Work

The COVID-19 pandemic has accelerated a trend that was already beginning to take hold: the shift to remote and hybrid work models. While many industries were forced to adopt remote work out of necessity, the long-term implications of this shift are profound. We're witnessing the redefinition of what the workplace looks like, and it's becoming clear that the traditional 9-to-5 office-based model may be a thing of the past for many industries.

Companies like Twitter, Shopify, and Facebook have announced permanent shifts to remote work for a significant portion of their workforce, while others are adopting hybrid models that blend in-office and remote work. This transformation has far-reaching implications for everything from real estate and urban planning to employee engagement and corporate culture.

With the rise of remote work comes the need for new tools and technologies to support collaboration, communication, and productivity. The development of virtual reality (VR) and augmented reality (AR) could play a pivotal role in bridging the gap between physical and virtual workspaces. Imagine virtual offices where employees can "meet" in a shared digital environment, complete with 3D representations of themselves and their colleagues, without the need to leave their homes.

Furthermore, the move to remote work is prompting a reassessment of global talent markets. Companies are no longer limited to hiring within a specific geographic area. The rise of global freelancing platforms like Upwork and Fiverr, combined with the ability to work from anywhere, means businesses can access a diverse pool of talent from around the world. For employees, this trend presents opportunities to work for companies across borders without the need for relocation, increasing flexibility and work-life balance.

The Green Economy and Sustainability Revolution

As the world grapples with the urgent need to address climate change, sustainability is becoming a key driver of innovation and economic growth. The green economy is no longer a niche sector; it's evolving into a core component of global markets. From renewable energy to sustainable agriculture, industries across the board are being transformed by the push for greener, more sustainable practices.

One of the most promising areas in this regard is the rise of clean energy technologies. Solar, wind, and hydroelectric power are becoming more cost-competitive with fossil fuels, and battery storage technology is rapidly improving, enabling more reliable and widespread adoption of renewable energy sources. Electric vehicles (EVs), driven by companies like Tesla and major automakers like General Motors and Ford, are expected to become the dominant mode of transportation within the next few decades.

The shift towards sustainability is not just about environmental responsibility; it also represents a significant economic opportunity. According to a report by the International Energy Agency (IEA), clean energy investments could create millions of jobs worldwide, particularly in sectors like manufacturing, construction, and technology development. The transition to a low-carbon economy could generate trillions of dollars in economic value, offering a powerful incentive for both governments and businesses to accelerate their green initiatives.

Moreover, consumer behavior is shifting as people become more conscious of the environmental impact of their purchases. Brands that prioritize sustainability are gaining a competitive edge, and companies that fail to adopt eco-friendly practices risk being left behind. The rise of circular economy models, where products are designed for reuse and recycling, is another trend gaining traction. For example, companies like Patagonia and IKEA are exploring ways to extend the life of their products through repair, resale, and recycling programs, catering to an increasingly eco-conscious customer base.

The Intersection of Biotechnology and Health

The biotech revolution is another trend poised to reshape the future. Advances in genetic engineering, CRISPR technology, and personalized medicine are transforming the healthcare landscape, offering new treatments and cures for diseases that were once considered untreatable. The COVID-19 pandemic underscored the importance of biotechnology, as pharmaceutical companies used mRNA technology to develop vaccines in record time.

In the future, biotechnology will play an even greater role in healthcare, not just in treating diseases but in preventing them. Personalized medicine, which tailors treatment to an individual's genetic makeup, is becoming more feasible thanks to breakthroughs in genomics and data analysis. This means that rather than prescribing a one-size-fits-all treatment, doctors will be able to offer customized therapies that are more effective and have fewer side effects.

Biotechnology is also making waves in areas beyond human health. Agricultural biotech, for instance, is helping to develop crops that are more resistant to pests, diseases, and climate change, offering solutions to the challenges of global food security. Meanwhile, synthetic biology, which involves redesigning organisms to perform new functions, is opening up possibilities for innovations ranging from biodegradable plastics to lab-grown meat, potentially revolutionizing entire industries.

5. The Rise of Decentralization: Blockchain and Beyond

Decentralization is another powerful trend that's gaining momentum, driven largely by the rise of blockchain technology. While blockchain is best known as the underlying technology behind cryptocurrencies like Bitcoin and Ethereum, its potential applications extend far beyond digital currencies. At its core, blockchain is a decentralized ledger system that allows for secure, transparent transactions without the need for intermediaries.

In the financial sector, blockchain is enabling faster, cheaper, and more secure transactions, and it's also powering the rise of decentralized finance (DeFi). DeFi platforms allow users to borrow, lend, and trade assets without the need for traditional banks or financial institutions, potentially disrupting the global financial system as we know it.

Blockchain's impact goes beyond finance. In supply chain management, blockchain can be used to track goods from production to delivery, ensuring transparency and reducing fraud. For example, Walmart has used blockchain to improve the traceability of its food supply chain, allowing the company to quickly identify the source of contamination in the event of a food safety issue.

Blockchain is playing a role in the rise of decentralized autonomous organizations (DAOs), which are organizations run by code and governed by members through blockchain-based voting mechanisms. These organizations operate without traditional management structures, offering a glimpse into a future where decentralized decision-making becomes the norm.

The Urgency of Trendspotting

In a rapidly changing world, identifying and understanding emerging trends is more critical than ever. The trends discussed—AI evolution, remote and hybrid work, the green economy, biotechnology, and decentralization—are just a few of the forces reshaping our future. As these trends converge, they will create new opportunities for innovation, economic growth, and societal transformation.

e ability to harness these trends requires more than just awareness. It demands a
)active mindset, a willingness to experiment, and the courage to make bold decisions in
: face of uncertainty. The leaders and organizations that succeed in tomorrow's world
l be those that can see beyond the immediate horizon, anticipate what's coming, and act
:isively to shape the future. As we look to tomorrow, the time to scan the horizon is now.

4. HOW TO SPOT WEAK SIGNALS, MEGATRENDS, AND THE DRIVERS OF CHANGE THAT WILL IMPACT INDUSTRIES AND MARKETS

In a world defined by rapid technological advancement, shifting consumer behavior and unpredictable geopolitical dynamics, the ability to spot weak signals, megatrends and the underlying drivers of change is more crucial than ever. These elements collectively serve as the foundation for strategic foresight, allowing businesses and industries to not only prepare for the future but actively shape it. Understanding how to identify these indicators of change can help organizations adapt more quickly, seize new opportunities, and remain competitive in the face of disruption. But what exactly are weak signals, megatrends, and drivers of change? And how can we, as individuals or businesses, hone our ability to recognize them before they fully materialize?

The Importance of Strategic Foresight

Strategic foresight is the practice of anticipating possible futures and understanding the factors that may lead us there. It's about looking beyond immediate concerns and current challenges to see the larger shifts that will reshape the environment in which we operate. Successful companies like Amazon, Google, and Tesla have all excelled at leveraging foresight to stay ahead of the curve, identifying and capitalizing on trends long before they become mainstream.

However, spotting future trends is not an exact science. The landscape of change is often murky, filled with weak signals that may not immediately appear relevant. The ability to detect these signals, differentiate them from noise, and connect them to larger megatrends and systemic drivers requires a mix of creativity, analytical thinking, and a broad understanding of global and local dynamics.

Weak Signals: Early Indicators of Change

Weak signals are subtle, fragmented pieces of information that suggest a possible future change but are not yet strong enough to predict an outcome with certainty. These signals often emerge from the periphery—areas of society, industry, or culture that may seem marginal or irrelevant at first glance. They might manifest in niche consumer behavior, early-stage technological innovations, or shifts in societal attitudes.

A classic example of a weak signal is the rise of remote work technologies, such as Zoom and Slack, before the COVID-19 pandemic. Prior to 2020, these tools were used primarily by tech-savvy companies or freelancers. However, for the vast majority of organizations, in-person work was still the norm. The pandemic served as an accelerator, transforming remote work from a weak signal into a mainstream reality. Companies that had previously recognized the potential of flexible work arrangements were better positioned to pivot and adapt during the crisis.

To spot weak signals, it's essential to cast a wide net and look for patterns in unexpected places. This often involves paying attention to early adopters, niche markets, and the fringes of societal and technological development. For example, in the world of retail, the rise of direct-to-consumer (DTC) brands such as Warby Parker and Glossier was a weak signal of a larger shift toward more personalized, digital-first shopping experiences. Early on, these brands seemed like anomalies in a landscape dominated by brick-and-mortar stores, but they ultimately foreshadowed a broader trend toward e-commerce and consumer empowerment.

Megatrends: The Forces Shaping the Future

While weak signals are the subtle, early-stage indicators of change, megatrends are the large-scale, long-term forces that have a more visible and profound impact on industries and markets. These are the powerful currents that shape the future, driving transformations in technology, economics, society, and the environment.

Megatrends often operate on a global scale, cutting across industries and regions. Unlike weak signals, which may be difficult to detect, megatrends are easier to identify because they are already shaping the world around us. However, understanding how they will evolve and intersect with other trends requires careful analysis and foresight.

One of the most significant megatrends today is the digital transformation of virtually every industry. The integration of digital technologies into business operations, from AI and machine learning to cloud computing and big data analytics, is reshaping how companies operate and deliver value. Businesses that fail to embrace digital transformation risk being left behind, as customers increasingly expect seamless, personalized, and tech-enabled experiences.

Another powerful megatrend is the demographic shift toward aging populations in many parts of the world. Countries like Japan, Germany, and the United States are experiencing a significant increase in the proportion of elderly citizens, which has wide-ranging implications for healthcare, labor markets, and consumer spending. As the population ages, industries such as healthcare, pharmaceuticals, and elder care will see increased demand, while other sectors, such as retail and real estate, will need to adapt to the changing needs and preferences of older consumers.

Similarly, climate change is a megatrend that will continue to reshape industries and markets in profound ways. The growing demand for sustainable products, renewable energy, and green technologies is not just a temporary shift in consumer behavior but a long-term transformation driven by both regulatory pressure and societal values. Companies that fail to prioritize sustainability may find themselves struggling to compete in a future where environmental responsibility is not just a preference but a necessity.

Drivers of Change: The Root Causes of Transformation

While weak signals and megatrends give us a sense of where the future is headed, it is essential to understand the underlying drivers of change—the root causes that are pushing these trends forward. Drivers of change are the deep, systemic forces that influence the evolution of industries, markets, and societies. They are often categorized into several key domains: technological, economic, environmental, social, and political.

Technological drivers are among the most significant forces of change in today's world. Innovations such as AI, blockchain, and 5G are not just altering individual industries but fundamentally changing the way we live and work. For example, the rise of AI is a driver of change that underpins many of the weak signals and megatrends we observe today. From automation in manufacturing to personalized medicine in healthcare, AI is enabling new levels of efficiency, customization, and innovation.

Economic drivers of change, such as globalization and shifting trade patterns, also play a critical role in shaping industries and markets. Global supply chains, once celebrated for their efficiency, have come under scrutiny due to disruptions caused by geopolitical tensions and the COVID-19 pandemic. As a result, we are seeing a resurgence of interest in local manufacturing and supply chain resilience, driven by the need for greater control and security in a volatile global landscape.

Environmental drivers of change, particularly those related to climate change, are exerting growing pressure on industries to adapt. The increasing frequency of extreme weather events, coupled with rising public awareness of environmental issues, is pushing businesses to adopt more sustainable practices. For example, the automotive industry is undergoing a profound transformation as companies shift from internal combustion engines to electric vehicles (EVs), driven by both regulatory mandates and consumer demand for greener alternatives.

Social drivers of change, such as shifting consumer values and demographic trends, also play a crucial role in shaping industries. The rise of the socially conscious consumer, particularly among younger generations, is forcing companies to rethink their business models. Brands that prioritize ethical sourcing, diversity, and environmental sustainability are gaining favor, while those that fail to align with these values may struggle to maintain customer loyalty.

political drivers, including regulatory changes, government policies, and geopolitical shifts, can also have a significant impact on industries. For example, the ongoing trade tensions between the United States and China are reshaping global supply chains and prompting companies to diversify their manufacturing bases. Similarly, regulatory changes related to data privacy, such as the European Union's General Data Protection Regulation (GDPR), are forcing companies to rethink how they collect, store, and manage consumer data.

Combining Weak Signals, Megatrends, and Drivers of Change

While it's helpful to understand weak signals, megatrends, and drivers of change individually, the real power lies in combining these elements to develop a more comprehensive view of the future. By connecting the dots between weak signals and megatrends, and understanding the drivers that are propelling them forward, businesses can gain deeper insights into where industries and markets are headed.

Consider the rise of electric vehicles (EVs) as an example. Ten years ago, the idea of electric cars replacing traditional gasoline-powered vehicles was still a weak signal, with only a handful of companies, like Tesla, pushing the boundaries of what was possible. Over time, however, this weak signal evolved into a megatrend as consumer interest in sustainability grew and governments began implementing stricter emissions regulations. The drivers of this change are multifaceted: technological advancements in battery storage, social drivers related to climate change awareness, and political drivers in the form of government incentives for EV adoption.

Another example can be seen in the healthcare industry, where the convergence of biotechnology, AI, and demographic shifts is reshaping the future of medicine. Weak signals, such as early-stage experiments in gene editing or AI-driven diagnostics, are now becoming more prominent, supported by the megatrend of aging populations and the increasing demand for personalized healthcare solutions. The drivers of change in this case include technological advancements in genomics and machine learning, as well as economic drivers such as rising healthcare costs and the need for more efficient care delivery models.

Practical Steps for Spotting Future Trends

Diversify Your Information Sources: To spot weak signals and understand megatrends, is essential to cast a wide net and look beyond your immediate industry. This could involve following academic research, monitoring startup ecosystems, attending conferences, or engaging with experts from different fields. The more diverse your information sources, the better equipped you will be to identify emerging trends.

Engage with Early Adopters and Innovators: Pay attention to what early adopters and innovators are doing, as they are often the first to pick up on weak signals. Whether it's a niche technology or a fringe social movement, early adopters can provide valuable insights into where things might be headed.

3. Use Scenario Planning: Scenario planning is a strategic tool that helps organization think through different possible futures. By considering multiple scenarios—each based o different combinations of weak signals, trends, and uncertainties—organizations can bett prepare for potential challenges and opportunities. This approach allows teams to visuali how various factors might interact and impact their objectives, fostering adaptability an strategic foresight.

Example: A global technology company might use scenario planning to prepare fo potential disruptions in the supply chain. They could develop three scenarios:

Scenario A: Supply chain remains stable, with steady demand for their products. Th company can focus on enhancing production efficiency and expanding its market share.

Scenario B: A major geopolitical event disrupts supply lines, leading to increased costs ar delays. The company might explore alternative suppliers, increase inventory, or adju pricing strategies to mitigate the impact.

Scenario C: Rapid advancements in technology lead to a shift in consumer preferenc towards more sustainable products. The company could invest in research ar development for eco-friendly alternatives and align its marketing strategies accordingly.

By preparing for these diverse scenarios, the company can create a robust strategic pl that addresses potential risks and leverages opportunities, ensuring resilience in a dynam environment.

Turning Foresight into Strategy: Building Resilient Organizations

In today's volatile, complex, and hyper-connected world, the ability to predict trends ar anticipate disruptions has become a necessity for organizational success. Howeve foresight alone is insufficient if it is not translated into tangible actions and embedde within a broader strategic framework. The most resilient organizations are not those th simply react to changes but those that proactively build their strategies around foresigh positioning themselves to not just survive but thrive in uncertainty. This chapter focuses how organizations can turn foresight into actionable strategies and build the kind resilience that not only withstands shocks but uses them as opportunities for growth.

Foresight: The Key to Anticipating Change

Foresight is about more than just predicting the future; it involves identifying emergi trends, analyzing potential risks, and envisioning various scenarios that could unfold. In era where change is the only constant, organizations must move beyond traditional, line methods of forecasting. Disruptive technologies, geopolitical shifts, changing consum behaviors, and environmental challenges all converge to create a future that is far le predictable than in the past.

...ke the example of Kodak. For decades, Kodak was a dominant player in the photography ...dustry, but despite its early foresight about the rise of digital photography, it failed to ...rn that knowledge into a successful strategy. Rather than fully embracing the digital ...nd, Kodak attempted to protect its existing film business. In contrast, companies like ...jifilm diversified their portfolios and expanded into areas such as medical imaging and ...smetics, leveraging their core competencies in chemicals and optics. This forward-...nking strategy allowed Fujifilm to build resilience, while Kodak struggled and ultimately ...ed for bankruptcy.

...ganizations that can turn foresight into strategy develop a dynamic capability that ...ables them to pivot quickly when new opportunities or threats arise. This means ...nstantly scanning the environment, understanding the implications of technological and ...cietal shifts, and making strategic bets based on a range of possible futures.

...e Role of Strategic Agility in Resilience

...ategic agility is a critical component of resilience. It refers to an organization's ability to ...pidly shift resources, structures, and processes in response to changing circumstances. ...lity is not just about being fast; it is about being adaptable, innovative, and responsive. ...s requires a mindset shift from rigid planning to flexible, iterative strategy development.

...nsider how Amazon has leveraged strategic agility to build resilience. When the ...mpany started as an online bookseller, its leadership could foresee the growth of e-...mmerce but did not limit themselves to one narrow market. Amazon's leadership, ...rticularly Jeff Bezos, employed foresight to recognize the broader potential of the ...ernet and e-commerce, while also having the strategic agility to pivot into different ...tors. The company rapidly expanded into electronics, cloud computing, and ...ertainment, continuously evolving its strategy based on emerging trends. This ability to ...ot, combined with its relentless focus on innovation, has allowed Amazon to remain a ...minant player across multiple industries.

... organizations to develop strategic agility, they must foster a culture that encourages ...perimentation and risk-taking. This involves empowering teams to make decisions ...ickly, removing bureaucratic barriers, and creating feedback loops that allow the ...ganization to learn from both successes and failures. A culture of agility ensures that ...en foresight identifies an emerging opportunity or threat, the organization is prepared ...act swiftly and decisively.

...bedding Foresight into Strategic Planning

...e of the most significant challenges organizations face is embedding foresight into the ...ategic planning process. Too often, strategic planning is treated as an annual exercise, ...connected from the fast-moving realities of the external environment. To build ...ilience, organizations must move away from rigid, long-term plans and embrace a more ...amic, scenario-based approach to strategy.

Scenario planning is a powerful tool that allows organizations to explore multiple potential futures and develop strategies that are robust across different outcomes. For example, Royal Dutch Shell has been using scenario planning since the 1970s to navigate the complex and unpredictable energy market. By envisioning various future scenarios ranging from fluctuating oil prices to environmental regulations—the company has been able to adjust its strategy and remain competitive in an industry that is constantly in flux.

Embedding foresight into strategic planning also means aligning foresight activities with the organization's broader vision and mission. It's not enough to have a team dedicated future-gazing; the insights generated from foresight activities must directly inform strategic decision-making at the highest levels. This requires a collaborative effort across departments, with leaders from different functions working together to interpret emerging trends and incorporate them into the overall strategy.

Building Resilience through Diversification and Innovation

Resilience is not just about surviving crises; it's about thriving in the face of adversity. One of the most effective ways to build organizational resilience is through diversification. When organizations diversify their product offerings, revenue streams, or markets, they reduce their exposure to any single risk. This creates a buffer that allows them to weather disruptions in one area while continuing to grow in others.

A prime example of resilience through diversification is the story of IBM. Once known primarily as a hardware company, IBM saw the decline of the personal computer market the late 1990s and early 2000s. Rather than clinging to its legacy business, IBM pivoted toward software, services, and cloud computing. The company's foresight, combined with its ability to execute a strategy focused on innovation and diversification, allowed it remain relevant in a rapidly changing tech landscape.

Innovation is another crucial element of resilience. Organizations that invest in innovation are better equipped to respond to disruptions and capitalize on new opportunities. Take the case of Tesla. Elon Musk's foresight regarding the future of sustainable energy, coupled with Tesla's relentless focus on innovation, has positioned the company as a leader not just in electric vehicles but in renewable energy solutions more broadly. By continuously pushing the boundaries of technology and rethinking traditional business models, Tesla built a level of resilience that enables it to withstand market fluctuations and regulatory challenges.

The Importance of Leadership in Driving Resilience

Resilient organizations are built on strong leadership. Leaders play a critical role in turning foresight into strategy, as they are responsible for setting the vision, fostering a culture innovation, and making the tough decisions that ensure long-term success. A resilient leader is someone who not only sees the future but can rally their organization around common purpose and inspire others to embrace change.

One of the key qualities of resilient leadership is the ability to balance short-term performance with long-term resilience. Leaders must be willing to make trade-offs between immediate results and investments in future growth. This requires courage and a willingness to take calculated risks. Consider how Satya Nadella transformed Microsoft. When he took over as CEO in 2014, Microsoft was struggling to adapt to the cloud computing revolution. Nadella's foresight about the future of technology, combined with his strategic focus on cloud services, enabled the company to regain its competitive edge. Today, Microsoft is a leader in cloud computing, and its resilience is a direct result of Nadella's forward-thinking leadership.

Leaders also need to communicate a clear vision of the future and engage their teams in the process of strategic planning. This involves creating a shared sense of purpose and ensuring that everyone in the organization understands how their role contributes to the broader strategy. When employees feel connected to the organization's mission and have a clear understanding of the future direction, they are more likely to embrace change and contribute to the organization's resilience.

The Role of Technology in Enhancing Organizational Resilience

In the digital age, technology plays a pivotal role in enhancing resilience. The rapid pace of technological innovation means that organizations must continuously adapt to new tools, platforms, and systems. However, technology is not just a challenge to be managed—it is a powerful enabler of resilience. Organizations that leverage technology effectively can streamline operations, improve decision-making, and create new value for customers.

One of the most significant technological advancements driving resilience is artificial intelligence (AI). AI enables organizations to analyze vast amounts of data, identify patterns, and make predictions with unprecedented accuracy. This foresight allows organizations to anticipate market shifts, optimize supply chains, and enhance customer experiences. For example, companies like Netflix use AI to analyze viewing data and predict customer preferences, allowing them to personalize content and stay ahead of competitors.

Digital transformation is a key driver of resilience. Organizations that embrace digital tools and platforms are better equipped to respond to disruptions and maintain continuity. The COVID-19 pandemic highlighted the importance of digital resilience, as companies that had already invested in digital infrastructure were able to pivot to remote work, e-commerce, and virtual services more easily than those that had not. Digital tools also enable organizations to scale rapidly, access new markets, and improve collaboration across teams.

Building a Resilient Future

In a world that is increasingly defined by uncertainty, building organizational resilience is not just a competitive advantage—it is a necessity for survival. Turning foresight into strategy is the cornerstone of resilience, enabling organizations to navigate change with agility, innovation, and foresight. By embedding foresight into strategic planning, fostering a culture of innovation, and leveraging technology, organizations can build the resilience needed to thrive in an unpredictable future.

Leadership plays a critical role in this process, as resilient leaders are those who can inspire their teams to embrace change and turn uncertainty into opportunity. As we move into the future, the most successful organizations will be those that not only anticipate change but proactively shape it through strategic foresight, agility, and innovation. The road ahead is uncertain, but for organizations that build resilience, the future holds limitless possibilities.

Integrating Foresight into Your Business Strategy to Foster Innovation, Adaptability, and Long-Term Success

In today's rapidly changing and complex business environment, integrating foresight into your business strategy is no longer a luxury but a necessity. Businesses that fail to look beyond the immediate horizon risk becoming obsolete, while those that leverage foresight to anticipate trends and disruptions set themselves on a path to innovation, adaptability, and long-term success. Foresight is not just about predicting the future, but about developing a mindset and strategy that allows businesses to stay ahead of the curve, seize new opportunities, and thrive amidst uncertainty. In this chapter, we explore how businesses can integrate foresight into their strategic frameworks and foster the innovation and adaptability needed to succeed in an unpredictable world.

Understanding the Power of Foresight

Foresight is a systematic process that enables organizations to envision multiple future scenarios, understand potential risks and opportunities, and prepare strategies to navigate them. It is not just about speculation but about rigorous analysis and strategic thinking. The best foresight practices involve gathering information from a wide array of sources—technological trends, social shifts, economic patterns, and geopolitical changes—and synthesizing these into actionable insights.

Consider the case of Netflix. In the early 2000s, the company foresaw the decline of DVD rentals and the rise of internet streaming. Rather than holding onto its original business model, Netflix made a bold pivot to digital streaming, investing in the technology and infrastructure needed to support it. This move not only saved the company from the fate that befell competitors like Blockbuster but turned Netflix into a global leader in digital entertainment. By using foresight to anticipate the future of media consumption, Netflix was able to innovate and build a business model that has continued to evolve alongside emerging technologies.

Similarly, Tesla leveraged foresight to foresee the growing demand for sustainable energy solutions. Long before electric vehicles (EVs) became mainstream, Tesla's leadership anticipated that the world would shift toward renewable energy due to increasing environmental concerns and regulatory pressures. By integrating this foresight into its strategy, Tesla was able to position itself as a leader in EV technology, while traditional car manufacturers lagged behind. Tesla's ability to innovate and adapt to future energy needs has not only driven its success but also reshaped the entire automotive industry.

Embedding Foresight into Your Strategic Framework

To foster innovation and adaptability, foresight must be embedded into the very fabric of an organization's strategic planning. This means moving beyond reactive approaches to strategy, which are often driven by short-term goals and immediate market pressures, and instead adopting a forward-thinking, proactive mindset. Strategic foresight requires continuous monitoring of emerging trends and the integration of those insights into decision-making processes at every level of the organization.

One practical approach to embedding foresight is through scenario planning. Scenario planning involves envisioning various potential futures and developing strategies that are robust across multiple outcomes. This technique helps businesses prepare for uncertainty by exploring different "what if" scenarios and ensuring that they have plans in place for a range of possible futures. Royal Dutch Shell has long been a pioneer of scenario planning, using it since the 1970s to navigate the complexities of the global energy market. Shell's ability to anticipate oil price fluctuations, geopolitical shifts, and environmental regulations has enabled it to remain a resilient and innovative player in the energy sector.

Embedding foresight also requires organizations to shift from rigid, long-term plans to more dynamic, flexible strategies. The traditional five-year strategic plan is no longer sufficient in an era where technological disruption and market volatility can render entire industries obsolete in a matter of months. Instead, businesses should adopt an iterative approach to strategy, regularly revisiting and adjusting their plans based on new information and changing circumstances. This kind of agile strategic planning allows organizations to quickly pivot when new opportunities or threats arise, ensuring that they remain competitive and innovative in the face of uncertainty.

Fostering a Culture of Innovation through Foresight

Foresight is a powerful tool for fostering a culture of innovation within an organization. When employees and leaders alike are encouraged to think about the future and consider the long-term implications of their actions, they are more likely to engage in creative problem-solving and experimentation. This forward-thinking mindset can drive the development of new products, services, and business models that are better aligned with emerging trends and customer needs.

Google is a prime example of an organization that has successfully integrated foresight into its culture of innovation. From its inception, Google has focused on identifying and developing future technologies, whether through its core search engine or through more speculative projects like self-driving cars, quantum computing, and artificial intelligence

(AI). Google's foresight-driven approach to innovation has allowed it to maintain a leading edge in the technology sector, continually evolving its offerings to meet the changing needs of users. The company's commitment to exploring future possibilities and investing in cutting-edge research has made it one of the most innovative organizations in the world.

Moreover, embedding foresight into your business strategy encourages risk-taking and experimentation—key drivers of innovation. When organizations actively seek to understand future trends and incorporate them into their strategies, they are more likely to embrace new ideas and take calculated risks. For example, Amazon's decision to launch Amazon Web Services (AWS) in 2006 was a risk at the time, but the foresight of recognizing the growing importance of cloud computing allowed the company to capture a new market and revolutionize enterprise IT infrastructure. Today, AWS is one of Amazon's most profitable divisions, illustrating how foresight, combined with a willingness to innovate, can lead to long-term success.

Enhancing Adaptability through Continuous Foresight

Adaptability is the ability to respond to changing conditions with agility and resilience, and it is a core element of long-term success in a volatile business environment. Businesses that integrate foresight into their strategy are better positioned to adapt because they have already anticipated potential changes and developed plans to address them.

One of the most effective ways to enhance adaptability is by adopting a continuous foresight process. Rather than treating foresight as a one-time exercise or an annual strategic planning task, businesses should integrate it into their day-to-day operations. This involves setting up systems to regularly collect and analyze data on emerging trends, customer preferences, competitive dynamics, and technological developments. By keeping an ongoing pulse on the future, businesses can quickly identify shifts in the market and adjust their strategies accordingly.

Consider the example of Zara, the global fast-fashion retailer. Zara's ability to adapt to rapidly changing fashion trends is a key driver of its success. The company has developed a highly responsive supply chain that allows it to quickly produce and deliver new clothing designs based on real-time data about customer preferences and emerging fashion trends. By continuously monitoring trends and integrating foresight into its operational strategy, Zara is able to stay ahead of competitors and meet the ever-changing demands of the fashion industry.

Another key aspect of adaptability is organizational flexibility. Businesses must be able to reallocate resources, restructure teams, and shift priorities in response to new information. This requires not only foresight but also a culture that values agility and experimentation. Companies like Slack have demonstrated this adaptability by pivoting their business models in response to market demands. Originally a gaming company, Slack's leadership used foresight to identify the growing need for communication tools in the workplace

...ding to its transformation into one of the most widely used collaboration platforms ...bally.

...ng Foresight to Identify Long-Term Opportunities

...resight not only helps businesses prepare for risks and challenges but also enables them ... identify long-term opportunities for growth and innovation. By looking beyond ...mediate market trends and considering the broader forces shaping the future, ...sinesses can uncover new markets, technologies, and business models that will drive ...ir success over the long term.

...e of the most significant opportunities on the horizon is the rise of artificial intelligence ...) and automation. Businesses that integrate foresight into their strategy are already ...paring for the transformative impact of AI on their industries. For example, healthcare ...anizations are using foresight to anticipate how AI will revolutionize diagnostics, ...atment planning, and patient care. By investing in AI-driven technologies today, these ...anizations are positioning themselves to lead in the future of healthcare.

...ilarly, the renewable energy sector offers long-term opportunities for businesses that ... foresight to anticipate the transition away from fossil fuels. Companies like Ørsted, a ...bal leader in offshore wind energy, have successfully integrated foresight into their ...ategy by shifting away from traditional oil and gas operations and investing heavily in ...ewable energy. Ørsted's foresight-driven approach has enabled it to capitalize on the ...wing demand for clean energy and become a leader in the global energy transition.

...resight also helps businesses identify opportunities to create new value for customers. ... instance, Procter & Gamble (P&G) has used foresight to anticipate shifts in consumer ...avior, particularly around sustainability. By integrating foresight into its product ...elopment strategy, P&G has been able to launch eco-friendly products and packaging ...utions that align with consumers' increasing desire for sustainable products. This not ...y enhances P&G's brand reputation but also drives long-term growth by meeting the ...lving needs of its customers.

...lding a Resilient Organization with Foresight

...ts core, foresight helps organizations build resilience. Resilience is the ability to not only ...hstand shocks and disruptions but also to adapt, innovate, and emerge stronger in the ... of challenges. Businesses that integrate foresight into their strategy are more likely to ...d resilience because they have a better understanding of potential risks and ...ortunities and can respond with agility and innovation.

...e the example of Toyota. The company has long been recognized for its resilience, ...ticularly in its ability to recover from supply chain disruptions. One key factor in ...ota's resilience is its use of foresight to anticipate potential risks and build redundancy ... its supply chain. After the 2011 earthquake and tsunami in Japan, which severely impacted Toyota's production capabilities, the company quickly adapted by leveraging foresight-driven supply chain strategy. Toyota's ability to anticipate disruptions a respond with flexibility allowed it to minimize the long-term impact of the disaster a continue to innovate in the automotive sector.

Ultimately, integrating foresight into your business strategy fosters a mindset continuous learning, innovation, and adaptability. It enables businesses to anticipate a respond to emerging trends, seize new opportunities, and build resilience in the face uncertainty. By embedding foresight into their strategic frameworks, businesses c position themselves for long-term success in an increasingly complex and unpredicta world.

Incorporating foresight into business strategy is not just about preparing for poten challenges but also about unlocking new opportunities for growth and innovation. developing the capability to anticipate future trends and disruptions, businesses can fos a culture of innovation, enhance their adaptability, and build resilience. Examples fr companies like Netflix, Tesla, and Zara demonstrate how foresight can lead transformative business models, agile strategies, and long-term success. As the busin environment continues to evolve, integrating foresight into your strategy will be a criti factor in staying ahead of the competition and achieving sustainable growth in the future

Key Aspect	Description	Example
Understanding Foresight	Systematic process to envision multiple future scenarios, anticipate risks, and seize opportunities.	Netflix pivoting to streaming to stay ahead of media consumption trends.
Embedding Foresight into Strategy	Incorporating foresight through scenario planning, flexible strategy, and regular updates to adapt to new information.	Shell's use of scenario planning to anticipate oil price changes and environmental regulations.
Fostering Innovation through Foresight	Encouraging creative problem-solving and risk-taking by aligning innovation with future trends and customer needs.	Google investing in future technologies like AI and quantum computing.
Enhancing Adaptability	Continuous foresight allows for rapid adaptation to changing conditions, supported by flexible structures and a dynamic strategy.	Zara's real-time trend monitoring enabling fast adaptation in the fashion industry.
Identifying Long-term Opportunities	Using foresight to explore emerging markets, technologies, and customer demands for sustained growth.	Tesla anticipating demand for electric vehicles, Procter & Gamble launching eco-friendly products.
Building Organizational Resilience	Foresight-driven strategies enable resilience by preparing for disruptions and building flexibility in business operations.	Toyota's foresight-driven supply chain resilience post-2011 earthquake.

FUTURE CHALLENGES QUESTIONS

1. How can businesses ensure that their foresight process is inclusive diverse perspectives to better predict global shifts and custom preferences?

2. What systems and technologies will businesses need to invest in to ma their foresight processes more data-driven and real-time responsive?

3. How can organizations balance short-term profit goals with long-ter foresight investments, especially in times of economic volatility?

5. CREATING A CULTURE OF FUTURE-THINKING: LEADERSHIP AND INNOVATION

In today's rapidly changing world, the ability to anticipate, adapt, and lead with a forward-thinking mindset has become essential. Organizations that cultivate a culture of future-thinking not only stay ahead of their competition but also inspire innovation and resilience. At the heart of this transformation lies leadership that is visionary, adaptable, and proactive. This leadership fosters innovation not as a reactionary measure, but as a core value, encouraging teams to think beyond the present and embrace the possibilities of tomorrow. In this essay, we will explore the key elements necessary to create a future-thinking culture, the role of leadership in driving innovation, and actionable strategies for embedding these principles into the very fabric of an organization.

Understanding Future-Thinking: The Foundation for Innovation

Future-thinking, also referred to as foresight or anticipatory leadership, is the ability to envision potential outcomes, challenges, and opportunities beyond the immediate future. It is not simply predicting the future, but rather preparing for various possible scenarios by developing a strategic mindset. The foundation of future-thinking is rooted in an openness to change, a curiosity about emerging trends, and a willingness to embrace uncertainty.

One of the most critical aspects of future-thinking is understanding that the world is increasingly interconnected. Globalization, technological advancements, and societal shifts are all converging to create a more complex and volatile business environment. For leaders, this means that decisions made today must be informed by an understanding of long-term impacts and potential disruptions. Future-thinking leaders ask questions such as: What trends are shaping the market? How will advancements in technology affect our industry in five to ten years? How can we prepare for shifts in consumer behavior or regulatory landscapes?

A practical example of future-thinking can be seen in the rise of renewable energy. Companies like Tesla and Google, years ahead of their competitors, anticipated the growing global emphasis on sustainability and environmental responsibility. By investing early in renewable energy solutions, they positioned themselves as leaders in this sector, paving the way for future growth. These organizations understood that the future demands more environmentally conscious solutions, and their early adoption of these principles not only set them apart but also influenced industry standards.

2. The Role of Leadership in Cultivating a Future-Thinking Culture

Leadership plays a pivotal role in fostering a culture of future-thinking within an organization. It begins with the leader's ability to inspire a shared vision, one that encourages employees to think beyond their current roles and projects. A future-thinking leader is one who is constantly scanning the horizon for new opportunities and potential threats, and who empowers their team to do the same.

Visionary leadership is more than just setting long-term goals; it involves actively engaging with the future. Leaders must foster an environment where employees are encouraged to innovate, take calculated risks, and explore new possibilities. This can be achieved through a variety of methods, including providing training on emerging trends, creating cross-functional teams that can collaborate on forward-looking projects, and rewarding employees who propose creative solutions to future challenges.

Leaders must also model future-thinking behaviors themselves. This means demonstrating curiosity about the future, engaging with new technologies, and showing a willingness to pivot when necessary. For example, Microsoft's CEO, Satya Nadella, is often cited as a future-thinking leader. Under his leadership, Microsoft shifted its focus from traditional software products to cloud computing and artificial intelligence, anticipating the growing demand for these technologies. This forward-looking approach has revitalized Microsoft's position in the tech industry and has set the company up for long-term success.

3. Encouraging Innovation through Future-Thinking

Innovation and future-thinking are inextricably linked. An organization that prioritizes future-thinking is more likely to be innovative, as its employees are encouraged to think creatively about how to solve future problems. Future-thinking provides the framework for innovation by identifying the gaps between where the organization is today and where it needs to be in the future.

One practical strategy for encouraging innovation is the creation of dedicated innovation teams or "labs" within the organization. These teams are tasked with exploring new ideas, experimenting with emerging technologies, and developing prototypes that can be tested and refined. By giving these teams the autonomy to explore future possibilities, organizations can ensure that they are staying ahead of the curve and are better prepared for potential disruptions.

Another key to fostering innovation is ensuring that employees have the resources they need to experiment and take risks. This includes providing access to the latest technology, offering training and development opportunities, and creating a safe environment where failure is seen as a learning opportunity rather than a setback. For example, 3M is known for its culture of innovation, where employees are encouraged to spend 15% of their time on personal projects. This freedom to experiment has led to the creation of some of the company's most successful products, including Post-it notes.

leaders must recognize that innovation often comes from collaboration and the cross-pollination of ideas. Encouraging collaboration across departments and disciplines can lead to breakthrough innovations that might not have been possible in a siloed environment. Leaders can facilitate this by creating spaces for open dialogue, where employees from different areas of the organization can share ideas and insights about future trends and challenges.

Embedding Future-Thinking into Organizational Culture

To create a lasting culture of future-thinking, it must be embedded into the very DNA of the organization. This means that future-thinking is not just the responsibility of leadership but is embraced at all levels of the organization. Every employee, regardless of their role, should feel empowered to contribute to the organization's future vision.

One way to embed future-thinking into organizational culture is through strategic foresight exercises, such as scenario planning. Scenario planning involves imagining different possible futures and developing strategies for each one. This exercise helps employees to think critically about the future and to consider the long-term implications of their decisions. By making scenario planning a regular part of the organization's strategic process, leaders can ensure that future-thinking becomes a core component of decision-making.

Another method is to incorporate future-thinking into the organization's values and mission statement. By explicitly stating a commitment to innovation and foresight, leaders signal to employees and stakeholders that these are priorities for the organization. For example, Amazon's mission to be "Earth's most customer-centric company" reflects a future-thinking mindset, as it focuses on anticipating and meeting the evolving needs of its customers.

Leaders can also promote future-thinking by creating opportunities for ongoing learning and development. This can include offering workshops on emerging trends, encouraging employees to attend conferences or enroll in courses on future-oriented topics, and fostering a culture of continuous learning. Google, for instance, is known for its emphasis on lifelong learning, offering employees access to a variety of educational resources and encouraging them to stay curious about new technologies and trends.

Overcoming Challenges in Creating a Future-Thinking Culture

While the benefits of a future-thinking culture are clear, creating and sustaining such a culture is not without its challenges. One of the biggest obstacles is resistance to change. Employees and even leaders may be hesitant to embrace future-thinking if they are accustomed to more traditional ways of doing things. To overcome this resistance, leaders must communicate the importance of future-thinking and demonstrate how it can lead to long-term success.

Another challenge is balancing short-term goals with long-term vision. While it is essen to plan for the future, organizations must also meet their immediate needs. Leaders c address this challenge by ensuring that future-thinking is integrated into everyc decision-making rather than treated as a separate initiative. This might involve setting bc short-term and long-term goals, with an understanding that achieving short-te objectives contributes to the overall future vision.

Future-thinking requires a level of comfort with uncertainty. Not every future scenario v play out as expected, and not every innovation will be successful. Leaders must be will to embrace ambiguity and to view failures as learning opportunities. This mindset can cultivated through open communication, where leaders share both successes and setba with their teams and encourage a culture of transparency.

Creating a culture of future-thinking requires visionary leadership, a commitment innovation, and a willingness to embrace change and uncertainty. Leaders who foste future-thinking culture empower their employees to think beyond the present and actively engage with the future. By encouraging innovation, facilitating collaboration, a embedding future-thinking into the organization's core values, leaders can ensure t their organization is prepared for whatever the future holds. The benefits of such a cult are clear: increased adaptability, sustained innovation, and a competitive edge in a rapi changing world.

The Role of Leadership in Nurturing a Forward-Thinking Mindset and Encouragin Culture That Embraces Change and Continuous Learning

In a world characterized by rapid technological advances, shifting markets, and evolv societal expectations, the importance of a forward-thinking mindset cannot be oversta Organizations that can anticipate and adapt to these changes are more likely to thr while those that resist transformation may quickly become obsolete. Central to adaptive capacity is leadership—visionary leaders who not only foresee the future but a nurture a culture that embraces change and promotes continuous learning. This es delves into the critical role leadership plays in fostering such a mindset and the strateg leaders can employ to build and sustain a culture that welcomes innovation, learning, a transformation.

1. Leadership as a Catalyst for Forward-Thinking

At its core, a forward-thinking mindset is about more than just predicting future trend encompasses a deeper strategic foresight—an understanding that the future is predetermined, and that leaders and their organizations must actively shape it. Leac who nurture a forward-thinking mindset inspire their teams to envision not only wha likely to happen but what could happen, encouraging them to be proactive in navigating unknown.

ne of the most notable examples of this is Jeff Bezos, the founder of Amazon. From its inception, Bezos led Amazon with a long-term, customer-centric vision. His approach was not merely about reacting to current trends but anticipating where technology and consumer behavior were heading. Bezos consistently encouraged his teams to think about the future, not just in terms of immediate profits but with an eye toward how the company could innovate to meet the evolving needs of its customers. This forward-thinking mindset is what drove Amazon to invest in technologies such as artificial intelligence, cloud computing, and even drone delivery—pioneering innovations that have kept the company at the forefront of its industry.

A forward-thinking leader also models curiosity and adaptability. Leaders who ask probing questions and challenge the status quo encourage their teams to adopt the same mindset. For example, in 2014, Satya Nadella took the helm as CEO of Microsoft. Under his leadership, Microsoft transformed from a company focused on traditional software products to one that embraced cloud computing, artificial intelligence, and open-source technologies. Nadella's curiosity and willingness to embrace new trends, paired with his emphasis on long-term thinking, helped to reverse Microsoft's stagnation and propel the company into a new era of growth and innovation.

Building a Culture That Embraces Change

While forward-thinking leaders play a crucial role in setting the vision for the future, the success of this vision hinges on the culture they cultivate. A culture that embraces change is one where employees are encouraged to experiment, challenge assumptions, and take calculated risks. Leaders must create an environment where change is seen as an opportunity for growth rather than a threat.

A key strategy for building such a culture is empowering employees to take ownership of change initiatives. Leaders must communicate that change is not something that happens to the organization but is driven by the organization. When employees feel that they are active participants in shaping the future, they are more likely to embrace change rather than resist it.

One example of this approach is seen at Google, where innovation is embedded in the company's DNA. Google encourages its employees to spend 20% of their time working on personal projects—an initiative that fosters creativity and allows employees to explore new ideas without fear of failure. This "20% time" led to the development of some of Google's most successful products, including Gmail and Google News. By giving employees the freedom to experiment and the autonomy to pursue their passions, Google has created a culture that thrives on change and innovation.

Leaders must also create a sense of psychological safety within their teams. Psychological safety, as defined by Harvard professor Amy Edmondson, is the belief that one will not be punished or humiliated for speaking up with ideas, questions, or concerns. In a psychologically safe environment, employees feel comfortable taking risks and embracing change, knowing that failure is not a career-ending mistake but a learning opportunity.

Pixar, the renowned animation studio, offers a prime example of this principle in action. The company's leadership, particularly co-founder Ed Catmull, has long emphasized the importance of candid feedback and constructive criticism. At Pixar, the "Braintrust" meetings allow filmmakers to present their work to a group of peers, who then provide honest feedback without fear of reprimand. This open, transparent approach to creative collaboration has allowed Pixar to push the boundaries of storytelling and animation, resulting in some of the most innovative films of the last two decades. By creating a culture of psychological safety, Pixar has been able to embrace change and innovation at every stage of the creative process.

3. Continuous Learning as a Pillar of Forward-Thinking Cultures

Change cannot be sustained without a commitment to continuous learning. In today's rapidly evolving world, organizations must prioritize learning as a core value. Leaders who encourage continuous learning create an environment where employees are not only open to new ideas but are actively seeking out new knowledge and skills to prepare for the future.

One of the most effective ways for leaders to promote continuous learning is by leading by example. When leaders themselves demonstrate a commitment to lifelong learning, they set the tone for the rest of the organization. This can be as simple as engaging in personal development activities, attending industry conferences, or taking courses in emerging fields. Leaders who remain curious and committed to their own growth inspire their teams to do the same.

An illustrative example is Bill Gates, co-founder of Microsoft. Even after stepping down from day-to-day operations at Microsoft, Gates has remained an avid learner, famously dedicating hours to reading and studying a wide range of topics. His passion for learning extends beyond his personal life and into his philanthropic efforts, where he consistently applies new knowledge to tackle global challenges such as poverty and disease. Gates' commitment to continuous learning has been a driving force behind his success, both in business and in his philanthropic endeavors.

Another strategy leaders can employ is creating formal learning and development programs within their organizations. These programs should go beyond traditional training and focus on equipping employees with the skills they need to thrive in an uncertain future. This might include offering courses on emerging technologies, leadership development programs, or opportunities for cross-functional collaboration.

One organization that has excelled in fostering a culture of continuous learning is IBM. Faced with the rapid pace of technological change, IBM recognized the need to reskill its workforce and prepare for the future. The company launched the IBM SkillsBuild platform providing employees with free access to training in areas such as data science, cybersecurity, and cloud computing. This initiative not only empowered employees to take control of their learning but also positioned IBM to remain competitive in a fast-changing industry.

Overcoming Resistance to Change

One of the greatest challenges leaders face in nurturing a forward-thinking mindset is overcoming resistance to change. Humans are naturally inclined to seek stability and security, and organizational change can often feel threatening. Leaders must be prepared to address this resistance and help their teams navigate the uncertainty that comes with embracing new ideas and ways of working.

One effective approach is to clearly communicate the reasons for change and the benefits it will bring. Employees are more likely to embrace change when they understand why it is necessary and how it will benefit them in the long run. Leaders should take the time to explain the organization's vision for the future and how each employee's role contributes to that vision.

For instance, when Adobe decided to transition from a traditional software licensing model to a subscription-based model, there was significant internal resistance. Many employees were concerned about how this shift would impact the company's revenue and their own job security. Adobe's leadership, however, took a transparent approach, clearly communicating the long-term benefits of the change and providing support for employees throughout the transition. This open dialogue helped to alleviate fears and allowed the company to make a successful shift to a more sustainable business model.

Leaders must also be patient and recognize that change takes time. Employees will not automatically adopt a forward-thinking mindset overnight, and there will inevitably be setbacks along the way. By providing ongoing support and celebrating small wins, leaders can gradually shift the organizational culture in a more forward-thinking direction.

Fostering Collaboration and Cross-Disciplinary Learning

Another critical component of a forward-thinking culture is collaboration. The most innovative ideas often emerge from the intersection of different perspectives, disciplines, and expertise. Leaders who encourage cross-disciplinary collaboration can unlock new possibilities and drive transformative change within their organizations.

A powerful example of this can be seen in the healthcare industry. As advancements in technology such as artificial intelligence and genomics continue to reshape the field, healthcare leaders are increasingly recognizing the value of collaboration between different sectors. Hospitals, tech companies, and research institutions are now working together to develop cutting-edge solutions that improve patient outcomes. By fostering a collaborative mindset, healthcare leaders are not only addressing today's challenges but also preparing for the future of medicine.

Leaders can encourage collaboration by creating opportunities for employees from different departments to work together on forward-thinking projects. This might involve forming cross-functional innovation teams, hosting hackathons, or establishing partnerships with external organizations to explore new possibilities. Collaboration, when combined with a forward-thinking mindset, can lead to breakthrough innovations that would not have been possible within a siloed structure.

Leadership plays a pivotal role in nurturing a forward-thinking mindset and creating culture that embraces change and continuous learning. By fostering curiosity, encouraging risk-taking, promoting psychological safety, and prioritizing learning, leaders can guide their organizations toward a future of innovation and growth. Through real-world examples, it is clear that leaders who embrace these principles are not only able to navigate the complexities of today's business environment but also to shape the future in profound ways. Ultimately, the organizations that succeed in the long run will be those that cultivate a forward-thinking culture—one that values learning, embraces change, and sees the future not as a threat, but as an opportunity.

APPENDICES

Appendix A: Strategic Foresight Tools and Resources

Strategic foresight is a crucial component for businesses aiming to rema competitive and relevant in an ever-evolving marketplace. As uncertainty grows global, political, technological, and economic spheres, organizations need relia tools and methodologies to anticipate and prepare for various future scenarios. In t appendix, we will explore a curated list of tools, software, and platforms desigr specifically for foresight analysis. These resources are practical, actionable, and have be proven to support organizations in envisioning future trends, identifying potential ris and capitalizing on opportunities.

1. Scenario Planning Software

Scenario planning is one of the most widely used tools in strategic foresight. This technic allows organizations to construct multiple plausible futures and test their strateg against these different possibilities. Popular scenario planning tools include:

- STRATForesight: This software offers a streamlined interface for creating detail complex scenario models. It is used by companies across various industries to simul multiple future environments based on economic, technological, and geopolitical facte With built-in analytics and visualization tools, STRATForesight enables businesses create dynamic reports and presentations that can inform leadership decision-making.

- Shaping Tomorrow: An AI-driven foresight platform that automates the generatior future scenarios based on vast quantities of data. It uses machine learning algorithms scan global news and reports, predicting trends and generating automated foresi analyses. Shaping Tomorrow is highly innovative and visionary, allowing organization stay ahead of emerging risks and trends without investing substantial time into man research.

2. Trend Identification Platforms

Understanding long-term trends is essential for future-proofing any organization. Tr identification platforms help businesses track evolving technologies, societal shifts, a economic changes, providing authoritative yet accessible insights into potential fut directions.

- TrendHunter: This platform offers an extensive database of consumer trends, provic insights on how societal values, technological advancements, and market demands evolving. Companies use TrendHunter to discover opportunities in emerging tren shaping their product development, marketing strategies, and overall business models. The tool is highly practical and actionable, offering users real-world examples of how these trends are manifesting in various industries.

The Future Today Institute (FTI) Tools: FTI offers a wide range of foresight tools, including their annual trend reports, which outline hundreds of technological and societal trends. FTI's methodology is rooted in rigorous data analysis, and their reports are highly respected across industries for their visionary, optimistic yet realistic outlook on future developments.

Data Visualization Tools

Data visualization plays a key role in transforming complex data into digestible and actionable insights. In the context of strategic foresight, visualization tools help organizations interpret large-scale trends and make sense of future possibilities.

Tableau: Widely regarded as one of the most comprehensive data visualization tools, Tableau allows users to create interactive, visual representations of data from various sources. In strategic foresight, companies use Tableau to visualize how different variables (such as technological advancements, market shifts, or geopolitical developments) could impact their business in the future. This helps them develop a more nuanced understanding of potential future scenarios and the factors driving them.

Kumu: Kumu is a platform designed to map complex systems and relationships. It's particularly effective for strategic foresight because it helps users visualize how different factors—such as stakeholders, trends, or challenges—are interconnected. Kumu's visualizations support organizations in understanding the complexity of future scenarios, helping them develop strategies that are robust and adaptive.

Horizon Scanning Tools

Horizon scanning is the process of detecting early signs of potentially important developments. The purpose of this tool is to identify weak signals—indications of emerging trends that may become significant in the future. This tool is essential for companies aiming to be proactive rather than reactive.

SenseMaker: SenseMaker is a horizon scanning and sense-making platform that combines qualitative and quantitative data analysis to identify emerging trends and weak signals. The tool is often used by governmental agencies, NGOs, and corporations to anticipate and respond to complex challenges. SenseMaker's innovative approach to data collection allows for the inclusion of human stories and narratives, which can provide rich insights into future developments that traditional data might miss.

Futures Platform: This tool combines expert foresight with AI to provide a comprehensive horizon-scanning solution. Futures Platform allows companies to explore potential future trends and assess their impact on their specific business context. It also provides collaborative environment where teams can work together to interpret the data an develop strategic responses.

In conclusion, strategic foresight tools and resources are designed to equip organizatior with the ability to anticipate future changes and adapt accordingly. These tools are not ju: practical but visionary, providing both high-level strategic insights and actionable ste[that can help businesses navigate an increasingly uncertain future.

Appendix B: Case Studies of Successful Future-Driven Organizations

Real-world examples are powerful learning tools that illustrate how foresight can k effectively applied to drive growth and innovation. In this appendix, we will explore ca: studies of organizations that have successfully integrated foresight into their strateg planning and operational processes. These companies demonstrate how proactive futu thinking can lead to significant competitive advantages.

1. Unilever: Leveraging Foresight for Sustainable Growth

Unilever is one of the world's largest consumer goods companies, with a diverse portfol of brands spanning from food to beauty products. Over the past decade, Unilever h increasingly used strategic foresight to guide its sustainability initiatives and long-ter business planning.

In 2010, Unilever launched its Sustainable Living Plan, a forward-thinking strategy aime at doubling the company's size while halving its environmental footprint by 2030. 1 achieve this ambitious goal, Unilever has consistently employed foresight tools to identi future trends related to sustainability, consumer behavior, and regulatory changes. F instance, the company's foresight team identified an emerging consumer preference f sustainable and ethically sourced products long before this trend became mainstream. I acting on this insight, Unilever was able to position its brands as leaders in sustainabili1 gaining a significant market advantage.

Through its foresight-driven approach, Unilever has not only achieved substantial busine growth but also earned recognition as a global leader in corporate sustainability. T company's story is an inspiring example of how foresight can be used to create a positiv future-driven strategy that aligns with both profitability and social responsibility.

2. Ford: Driving Innovation Through Scenario Planning

Ford Motor Company has been a pioneer in utilizing strategic foresight to navigate t rapidly changing automotive industry. Faced with disruptive forces such as elect vehicles, autonomous driving technologies, and changing consumer preferences, Ford recognized the need to look ahead and prepare for multiple possible futures.

Ford's scenario planning process has been instrumental in helping the company anticipate and respond to these industry shifts. One notable example is the company's foresight work on the future of mobility. As early as 2014, Ford foresaw the rise of ride-sharing services and urban mobility solutions, which led them to invest in Ford Smart Mobility, an initiative aimed at developing innovative transportation solutions for the future.

By leveraging scenario planning, Ford was able to position itself as a forward-thinking company that embraces innovation rather than reacting to market changes. This foresight-driven approach has allowed the company to remain relevant in an industry undergoing rapid transformation.

Shell: Navigating Uncertainty Through Strategic Foresight

Shell, one of the largest oil and gas companies in the world, has been using foresight for decades to help guide its long-term strategies. The company's Shell Scenarios program is one of the most well-known examples of scenario planning in the corporate world. Since the 1970s, Shell has used scenarios to explore possible futures, ranging from technological advancements to geopolitical shifts, allowing them to navigate uncertainty with greater confidence.

In recent years, Shell has used foresight to address the growing global emphasis on renewable energy. The company's scenarios have helped it anticipate how the energy landscape might evolve and what role oil and gas will play in a world increasingly focused on sustainability. By exploring these alternative futures, Shell has been able to diversify its energy portfolio, investing heavily in renewables and energy transition technologies.

Shell's use of foresight illustrates how even industries facing significant disruption can use future-driven thinking to adapt and thrive.

Appendix C: Glossary of Key Terms in Strategic Foresight

Strategic foresight is a critical discipline for organizations, enabling them to plan for the future in an informed, structured manner. It involves a wide range of concepts and methodologies that help businesses, governments, and individuals anticipate change, mitigate risks, and leverage opportunities in uncertain futures. Understanding the key terms in foresight is essential for engaging effectively with the field and applying its principles in a practical, actionable way.

Strategic Foresight

Definition: Strategic foresight is the process of systematically exploring possible futures to inform decision-making in the present. It involves identifying trends, imagining different scenarios, and using these insights to create flexible strategies that help organizations navigate uncertainty.

Example: A tech company might use strategic foresight to explore how artificial intelligence and automation could transform their industry over the next 20 years. By examining various scenarios, the company can identify potential opportunities to innovate and adapt their business model to future demands.

2. Scenario Planning

Definition: Scenario planning is a foresight tool that helps organizations imagine and evaluate different future environments. It involves creating detailed narratives or scenarios based on combinations of key drivers, such as political, economic, or technological factors. The goal is to test how strategies might perform under different circumstances.

Example: A multinational energy company might create scenarios where renewable energy becomes dominant, oil prices plummet, or geopolitical tensions disrupt supply chains. By preparing for these potential futures, the company can build resilient strategies that remain effective across a wide range of possibilities.

3. Horizon Scanning

Definition: Horizon scanning is the process of detecting early signs of emerging trends disruptions. It involves systematically monitoring sources of information, such as news reports, academic papers, and expert opinions, to identify "weak signals" that may indicate important future developments.

Example: A pharmaceutical company might engage in horizon scanning to detect early stage scientific breakthroughs in biotechnology, which could revolutionize their drug development process. By acting on these signals before competitors, the company gains first-mover advantage.

4. Weak Signals

Definition: Weak signals are subtle indications of potential future developments. They are often overlooked or dismissed as irrelevant, but when recognized and analyzed, they can provide early warnings of significant change.

Example: In the early 2000s, the rise of online social networking platforms like Friendster and MySpace was a weak signal for the eventual dominance of social media communication, marketing, and business. Companies that spotted these signals early were better positioned to leverage platforms like Facebook and Twitter as they grew.

Trend Analysis

Definition: Trend analysis is the practice of examining historical data and current developments to identify patterns and predict future changes. Trends can be social, technological, economic, environmental, or political (often referred to as STEEP trends), and understanding them helps organizations forecast possible future trajectories.

Example: An automotive company might analyze the trend toward urbanization and the growing demand for electric vehicles. By understanding this shift, they can prioritize the development of electric models that meet the needs of eco-conscious, city-dwelling consumers.

Megatrends

Definition: Megatrends are large-scale, global forces that shape the future over extended periods, typically spanning decades. They are often slow-moving but have significant and lasting impacts across industries and regions.

Example: Climate change is a megatrend affecting almost every sector, from agriculture to energy to finance. Companies and governments worldwide are adapting their strategies to mitigate risks and capitalize on opportunities arising from the transition to a low-carbon economy.

Drivers of Change

Definition: Drivers of change are the underlying forces that influence or shape future developments. They can be internal, such as changes within an organization, or external, like economic shifts, technological innovations, or societal changes.

Example: The rapid advancement of artificial intelligence is a driver of change in industries like healthcare, where AI-driven diagnostics and personalized medicine are transforming the way diseases are treated.

Wild Cards

Definition: Wild cards are low-probability, high-impact events that can dramatically alter the future. They are often unexpected and can either be catastrophic or provide unique opportunities.

Example: The COVID-19 pandemic is a wild card that disrupted global economies, supply chains, and societal norms. While it caused widespread challenges, it also accelerated digital transformation, with many industries embracing remote work, e-commerce, and automation at unprecedented speeds.

9. Visioning

Definition: Visioning is a strategic foresight method where organizations collaboratively develop a desired future state. It involves imagining a preferred future and working backward to identify the steps necessary to achieve it.

Example: A city might engage in a visioning exercise to create a sustainable urban development plan. Stakeholders—including government officials, business leaders, and citizens—work together to define what a "smart, green city" looks like in 20 years and outline policies, infrastructure projects, and innovations needed to realize that vision.

10. Backcasting

Definition: Backcasting is the process of starting with a desired future outcome and working backward to the present, identifying the actions needed to achieve that future. It is often used in sustainability planning and policy development.

Example: A government aiming for a carbon-neutral economy by 2050 might use backcasting to map out the necessary steps, such as investing in renewable energy, promoting electric vehicles, and phasing out fossil fuels.

11. Systems Thinking

Definition: Systems thinking is an approach to understanding complex systems by recognizing the interrelationships between various components. In strategic foresight, systems thinking helps organizations see how different drivers, trends, and factors influence one another, enabling more comprehensive future planning.

Example: A food company might use systems thinking to examine how climate change, water scarcity, and agricultural innovation are interconnected. By considering these relationships, the company can develop more sustainable supply chain strategies that are resilient to future environmental pressures.

12. Disruptive Innovation

Definition: Disruptive innovation refers to technological advancements or business models that radically change industries, often displacing established players and reshaping markets.

Example: The advent of streaming services like Netflix disrupted the traditional television and movie industries by offering on-demand content. Companies that recognized disruptive innovation early were able to adapt, while others, such as Blockbuster, were left behind.

3. Strategic Agility

Definition: Strategic agility is the ability of an organization to quickly and effectively adapt to changes in the external environment. It involves flexible decision-making processes, a willingness to pivot when necessary, and the capacity to capitalize on emerging opportunities.

Example: When COVID-19 hit, many retailers with strong online infrastructures were able to pivot rapidly to e-commerce, gaining a competitive edge. Companies with strategic agility were better able to adapt to the new realities of consumer behavior, while others struggled to survive.

4. Black Swan Events

Definition: A Black Swan event is a rare and unpredictable event with severe consequences. While often considered unforeseeable, the term highlights the limitations of traditional risk management approaches that rely on past data to predict future events.

Example: The 2008 global financial crisis is considered a Black Swan event, as it was largely unforeseen by most financial institutions, yet its impact was devastating and widespread, affecting economies worldwide.

5. Futures Literacy

Definition: Futures literacy refers to the capacity to understand, anticipate, and shape the future by leveraging foresight tools and methods. It is a critical skill for individuals and organizations navigating uncertainty.

Example: A CEO with strong futures literacy might use foresight tools like scenario planning and trend analysis to anticipate market shifts and guide their company toward sustainable growth in an increasingly volatile world.

6. Delphi Method

Definition: The Delphi Method is a structured communication technique used in foresight to gather expert opinions on future developments. Through a series of surveys or rounds, experts provide feedback on key trends or uncertainties, and their responses are aggregated to form a consensus.

Example: A think tank might use the Delphi Method to gather expert predictions on the future of renewable energy, enabling them to produce a report that helps governments and businesses make informed decisions about long-term energy investments.

17. PESTLE Analysis

Definition: PESTLE (Political, Economic, Social, Technological, Legal, Environmental) analysis is a strategic tool used to examine the macro-environmental factors that could impact an organization's future.

Example: An airline might conduct a PESTLE analysis to evaluate how emerging technologies (e.g., electric planes), legal regulations (e.g., emissions standards), and social attitudes toward air travel (e.g., increased demand for sustainable tourism) could affect their long-term business strategy.

18. Corporate Foresight

Definition: Corporate foresight is the practice of embedding foresight methodologies into an organization's strategic planning process to anticipate future challenges and opportunities, enabling better decision-making.

Example: Siemens, a multinational conglomerate, incorporates corporate foresight into its innovation strategy by continuously exploring technological trends, such as automation and digitalization, ensuring it remains at the forefront of industry advancements.

19. Anticipatory Governance

Definition: Anticipatory governance refers to the use of foresight and future planning in policymaking to ensure that governments are prepared for long-term challenges and opportunities.

Example: Singapore is known for its anticipatory governance, using strategic foresight to plan for issues like climate change, aging populations, and technological disruption. This approach helps the government make proactive decisions rather than reacting to crises as they arise.

20. Causal Layered Analysis (CLA)

Definition: Causal Layered Analysis is a foresight method that explores different levels of understanding about an issue or future scenario. It examines the surface-level trends, underlying systemic factors, and deeper cultural worldviews that shape our perceptions of the future.

Example: In exploring the future of urban transportation, CLA might look at surface trends like the rise of electric vehicles, systemic issues such as urban congestion, and deeper cultural narratives around mobility and freedom, leading to a more comprehensive understanding of the future of transportation.

These terms are foundational to understanding and engaging with the field of strategic foresight. By mastering the language of foresight, organizations can better anticipate and navigate the complexities of the future, ensuring that they remain resilient and adaptive in a rapidly changing world. Through tools like scenario planning, horizon scanning, and trend analysis, foresight empowers decision-makers to move beyond reactive strategies and proactively shape the future in line with their goals and values.

END

www.ingramcontent.com/pod-product-compliance
Lightning Source LLC
Chambersburg PA
CBHW051532240526
45471CB00019B/957